Consolidation in the Data Center
Simplifying IT Environments to Reduce Total Cost of Ownership

David Hornby and Ken Pepple

Sun Microsystems Press
A Prentice Hall Title

The publisher offers discounts on this book when ordered in bulk quantities. For more information, contact: Corporate Sales Department, Phone: 800-382-3419; Fax: 201-236-7141; E-mail: corpsales@prenhall.com; or write: Prentice Hall PTR, Corp. Sales Dept., One Lake Street, Upper Saddle River, NJ 07458.

Editorial/production superviser: *Nicholas Radhuber*
Cover design director: *Jerry Votta*
Cover designer: *Kavish & Kavish Digital Publishing & Design*
Manufacturing manager: *Alexis R. Heydt*
Marketing manager: *Debby vanDijk*
Acquisitions editor: *Gregory G. Doench*

Sun Microsystems Press
Publisher: *Michael Llwyd Alread*

10 9 8 7 6 5 4 3 2 1

ISBN 0-13-045495-8

Sun Microsystems Press
A Prentice Hall Title

Acknowledgements

It's difficult to acknowledge everyone who was part of this book. But our thanks certainly go to the following:

Julie Snow for her excellent editing skills and her ability to keep us plugging along. Gary Rush and the other folks with the Sun BluePrints™ program for letting us write and publish this book. Ken Buchanan and Tom Bankert for understanding the importance of data center consolidation, and supporting our efforts to develop much of the methodology we describe in this book. Jerry Mays for his project management expertise. Bill Walker for helping us through the process of submitting the idea to the Sun BluePrints program, and for supporting our efforts. Torrey McMahon for his expertise in storage consolidation. Our reviewers, Auyong Chaun, KC Fung, Shyam Mittur, and Dennis Walker for taking their own time to edit and make comments about this book.

Consolidation has been an ongoing effort for Sun Professional Services (Sun PS) for the past four years. Our thanks goes out to the many fine people in Sun PS and in Sun Microsystems, Inc. for their expertise and support. This book wouldn't be possible without them.

Acknowledgements from David Hornby: I would also like to thank the following people. Coauthoring this book would have been impossible without the support of my manager, Dave O'Connor. I found out the hard way that writing a book takes a lot of time and effort, and Dave helped make that time available. Thanks to my wife, Lorna, for supporting my writing efforts. Her ongoing support and encouragement have been invaluable.

Acknowledgements from Ken Pepple: I would also like to thank Tom Yap and Kim Rogers for allowing me to spend the better part of six months working on this book. Thanks to Joe Rich from TeamQuest Corporation for his generous support and expertise with his company's products, and to Joost Pronk van Hoogeveen for providing great information about the new features of the Solaris™ 9 Resource Manager and resource management in general. Thank you to my mother, Joan Randall, for encouraging me to chase my dreams, no matter where they lead; and to my father, David Pepple, for buying my first compiler, even though it ran on an IBM PCjr. Last, but not least, I would like to thank Shelley Mitchell and my dog, Zeke, for putting up with my early morning calls from distant countries when I was away, and for putting up with incessant late night typing when I was home.

Contents

Preface

This Sun BluePrints book provides a methodology for justifying, scoping, and implementing server and storage consolidation. This book addresses the following topics:

- Establishing a vision for server consolidation
- Methods for achieving and measuring a successful solution
- Understanding and creating a business case for a consolidation project
- Quantifying total cost of ownership (TCO) savings and other benefits of consolidation
- Designing an architecture for a consolidated solution
- Implementing server consolidation based on the established vision
- Managing a consolidated solution

Sun BluePrints Program

The mission of the Sun BluePrints program is to empower Sun customers with the technical knowledge required to implement reliable, extensible, and secure information systems within the data center using Sun products. This program provides a framework to identify, develop, and distribute best practices information that applies across the Sun product lines. Technical subject matter experts in various areas contribute to the program, and focus on the scope and usefulness of the information.

The Sun BluePrints program includes books, guides, and online articles. Through these vehicles, Sun can provide guidance, installation and implementation experiences, real-life scenarios, and late-breaking technical information.

The monthly electronic magazine, Sun BluePrints OnLine, is located on the web at http://www.sun.com/blueprints. To be notified about updates to the Sun BluePrints program, please register yourself on this site.

Who Should Use This Book

The audience for this Sun BluePrints book includes customers and partners interested in server and storage consolidation, mixed workload planning and management, and TCO analysis for production environments. Specifically, this book is for data center managers, chief architects, and executive-level information technology (IT) managers.

Before You Read This Book

This book complements the *Resource Management and Capacity Planning* Sun BluePrint. It provides a high-level analysis of some of the topics and products presented in *Resource Management and Capacity Planning*, and cross-references this material, when necessary. You may find it helpful to review the *Resource Management and Capacity Planning* Sun BluePrints book before reading this book.

How This Book Is Organized

This book contains the following chapters.

Chapter 1, "Evolution of the Data Center" provides a definition of consolidation and explains how data centers have evolved to a point where consolidation has become necessary.

Chapter 2, "Business Aspects of Consolidation" explains the business issues to consider when preparing for a consolidation project. This chapter provides guidance for selling a consolidation project, provides methods for properly assessing the cost of complexity and total cost of ownership, and explains how you can avoid some of the problems you may face during a consolidation project.

Chapter 3, "Types of Consolidation" describes the different types of consolidation you can perform. This chapter provides specific information about the opportunities of each type of consolidation, and presents general strategies used to perform them.

Chapter 4, "Consolidation Methodology" introduces the four phases of Sun Professional Services' consolidation methodology, and identifies general recommendations for their successful completion.

Chapter 5, "Performing a Consolidation Feasibility Study" explains the value of performing a feasibility study, and provides guidance for doing so.

Chapter 6, "Planning a Consolidation Project" explains the importance of properly planning for a consolidation project. Through the use of a sample project, this chapter explains the tasks involved in creating a project plan including defining objectives, estimating time lines, setting milestones, and estimating realistic project durations. In addition, this chapter provides information about identifying and securing essential project resources.

Chapter 7, "Assessing Technical Feasibility" explains how to perform the tasks that must be completed before you can design a consolidated architecture. These tasks include compiling a starting inventory, profiling applications, assessing requirements (of platforms, storage, networks, security, and infrastructure and operations), and assessing risk.

Chapter 8, "Designing a Consolidated Architecture" explains how to perform the tasks involved in designing a consolidated architecture. These tasks include reviewing requirements, developing an initial solution, prototyping the design, revising the design, and documenting the architecture.

Chapter 9, "Implementing a Consolidated Solution" explains how to specify the low-level details of the platform, define a migration strategy, build the consolidated environment, and deploy it. Also, it provides information about putting the solution into production and ensuring that the administrative staff is trained and prepared to document the results of the consolidation.

Chapter 10, "Managing a Consolidated Environment" explains some of the sticky operational issues created by the newly consolidated solution. With several applications sharing the same platform and operating systems infrastructure, availability, and maintenance problems are bound to arise. This chapter explains the importance of careful planning, strong operational processes, and flexible architectures in facing these challenges.

Appendix A presents the complete sample feasibility study referenced in Chapter 5.

Appendix B presents a sample application profile.

Ordering Sun Documents

You can view, print or purchase a broad selection of Sun documentation, including localized versions, at: `http://www.sun.com/documentation`.

Accessing Sun Documentation Online

The `docs.sun.com`sm web site enables you to access Sun technical documentation online. You can browse the `docs.sun.com` archive, or search for a specific book title or subject. The URL is `http://docs.sun.com/`.

## CHAPTER 1

Evolution of the Data Center

The need for consolidation in the data center didn't just occur overnight; we have been building up to it for a long time. In this chapter, we review the evolution of today's data center and explain how we have managed to create the complex information technology (IT) environments that we typically see today.

This chapter presents the following topics:

- "Consolidation Defined" on page 1
- "History of the Data Center" on page 2
- "Complexity in the Data Center" on page 6

Consolidation Defined

According to *Webster's College Dictionary*, consolidation is the act of bringing together separate parts into a single or unified whole. In the data center, consolidation can be thought of as a way to reduce or minimize complexity. If you can reduce the number of devices you have to manage, and if you can reduce the number of ways you manage them, your data center infrastructure will be simpler. With a simpler infrastructure, you should be able to manage your data center more effectively and more consistently, thereby reducing the cost of managing the data center and reducing your total cost of ownership (TCO).

When we first started working on consolidation methodologies in 1997, we focused on server and application consolidation; the goal was to run more than one application in a single instance of the operating system (OS). Since then, the scope has widened to the point that virtually everything in the corporate IT environment is now a candidate for consolidation, including servers, desktops, applications, storage, networks, and processes.

History of the Data Center

Over the last 40 years, the data center has gone through a tremendous evolution. It really wasn't that long ago that computers didn't exist. To better understand how we got to a point where consolidation has become necessary, it's worth taking a look at the evolution of today's computing environment.

The following sections address the role mainframes, minicomputers, and distributed computing systems have played in the evolution of the data center in a historical context. However, it is important to note that many of the qualities mentioned affect the choices IT architects make today. While mainframes are still the first choice of many large corporations for running very large, mission-critical applications, the flexibility and affordability of other options have undoubtedly altered the design and functionality of data centers of the future.

The Role of Mainframes

Mainframes were the first computers to gain wide acceptance in commercial areas. Unlike today, when IBM is the sole remaining mainframe vendor, there were several mainframe manufacturers. Because IBM has always been dominant in that arena, the major players were known as IBM and the BUNCH (Burroughs, Univac, NCR, Control Data, and Honeywell). These major players dominated the commercial-computing market for many years, and were the data processing mainstay for virtually all major U.S. companies.

The Strength of Mainframes

The strengths of mainframes make them valuable components to nearly every large-scale data center. These strengths include:

- **Power.** For many years, mainframes were the most powerful computers available, and each new generation got bigger and faster. While the power and performance of distributed computing systems have improved dramatically over the past several years, mainframes still play an important role in some data centers.

- **High utilization rates.** Because of the expense involved in purchasing mainframes and building data centers to house them, mainframe users tend to use every bit of available computing power. It's not uncommon to find mainframes with peak utilization rates of over 90 percent.

- **Running multiple applications through workload management.** Because of the large investment required to purchase mainframes, it is important for companies to able to run multiple applications on a single machine.

To support multiple applications on a single system, mainframe vendors, especially IBM, developed the concept of workload management. Through workload management, you can partition a mainframe and allocate its computing resources such that each application is guaranteed a specific set of resources. This ability allows corporate IT departments to provide their customers with very high application availability and very high service levels.

There is no doubt that mainframes are today's champions of workload management. This isn't surprising since this capability has been evolving over the last 30 years. For example, you can expect a fully implemented, highly evolved workload-management system to manage:

- Central processing unit (CPU) usage

- Dispatch priority

- Storage used

- Input/output (I/O) priority

Some workload managers have end-to-end management functions that monitor what is happening in the application and in the database, and that balance transaction workloads across multiple application and database regions.

- **Well-defined processes and procedures.** Because of their size, as well as their high cost, mainframes are run in data centers where specific processes and procedures can be used for their management. The IT environments that house mainframes are generally highly centralized, making it fairly easy to develop very focused policies and procedures. As a result, audits of mainframe environments usually show highly disciplined computing environments—a quality that further contributes to the mainframe's ability to deliver high service levels.

The Problem With Mainframes

While mainframes provide the power and speed customers need, there are some problems with using them. These problems include:

- **Financial expense.** The biggest drawback of using mainframes is the expense involved in purchasing, setting up, and maintaining them. When you exceed the capacity of a mainframe and have to buy another, your capital budget takes a big hit. For many years, mainframe manufacturers provided the only computing alternative available, so they priced their hardware, software, and services accordingly. The fact that there was competition helped somewhat, but because vendors had their own proprietary OSs and architectures, once you chose one and began implementing business-critical applications, you were locked in.

- **Limited creative license.** In addition to their high cost, the inflexible nature of the processes and procedures used to manage mainframe environments sometimes limits the methods developers use to develop and deploy applications.

- **Increased time-to-market.** Historically, the length of mainframe development queues was measured in years. In this environment, the ability of a business to change its applications or to deploy applications to meet new market needs may be severely limited.

As a result of the preceding characteristics, and as new alternatives have been made available, many businesses have moved towards faster and cheaper platforms to deliver new applications.

The Introduction of Minicomputers

During the 1970s and 1980s, minicomputers (minis) became an attractive alternative to mainframes. They were much smaller than mainframes, and were much less expensive. Designed as scientific and engineering computers, minis were adapted to run business applications. The major players in this market were DEC, HP, Data General, and Prime.

Initially, companies developed applications on minis because it gave them more freedom than they had in the mainframe environment. The rules and processes used in this environment were typically more flexible than those in the mainframe environment, giving developers freedom to be more creative when writing applications. In many ways, minis were the first step towards freedom from mainframe computing.

While this new found freedom was welcomed by many, minis had two significant deficiencies. First, because minis were small and inexpensive, and didn't need specialized environments, they often showed up in offices or engineering labs rather than in traditional data centers. Because of this informal dispersion of computing assets, the disciplines of mainframe data centers were usually absent. With each computer being managed the way its owner chose to manage it, a lack of accepted policies and procedures often led to a somewhat chaotic environment. Further, because each mini vendor had its own proprietary OS, programs written for one vendor's mini were difficult to port to another mini. In most cases, changing vendors meant rewriting applications for the new OS. This lack of application portability was a major factor in the demise of the mini.

The Rise of Distributed Computing

After minis, came the world of distributed systems. As early users of UNIX™ systems moved out of undergraduate and postgraduate labs and into the corporate world, they wanted to take the computing freedom of their labs into the commercial world, and as they did, the commercial environment that they moved into evolved into today's distributed computing environment.

One important characteristic of the distributed computing environment was that all of the major OSs were available on small, low-cost servers. This feature meant that it was easy for various corporate groups (departments, work groups, etc.) to purchase servers outside the control of the traditional, centralized IT environment. As a result, applications often just appeared without following any of the standard development processes. Engineers programmed applications on their desktop workstations and used them for what later proved to be mission-critical or revenue-sensitive purposes. As they shared applications with others in their departments, their workstations became servers that served many people.

While this distributed environment provided great freedom of computing, it was also a major cause of the complexity that has led to today's major trend towards consolidation.

UNIX Operating System

During the late 1960s, programmers at AT&T's Bell Laboratories released the first version of the UNIX OS. It was programmed in assembly language on a DEC PDP-7. As more people began using it, they wanted to be able to run their programs on other computers, so in 1973, they rewrote UNIX in C. That meant that programs written on one computer could be moved easily to another computer. Soon, many vendors offered computers with the UNIX OS. This was the start of the modern distributed computing architecture.

Although the concept of portable UNIX programs was an attractive one, each vendor enhanced their own versions of UNIX with varying and diverging features. As a result, UNIX quickly became Balkanized into multiple incompatible OSs. In the world of commercial computing, Sun became the first of today's major vendors to introduce a version of UNIX with the SunOS™ system in 1982. Hewlett-Packard followed soon thereafter with HP-UX. IBM didn't introduce their first release of AIX until 1986.

Although Linux and Windows NT are growing in popularity in the data center, UNIX remains the most common and most highly developed of these OSs. It is the only major OS to adequately support multiple applications in a single instance of the OS. Workload management is possible on UNIX systems. Although they are not yet in the mainframe class, the UNIX system's current workload management features provide adequate support for consolidation.

Complexity in the Data Center

All of this freedom to design systems and develop applications any way you want has been beneficial in that it has allowed applications to be developed and released very quickly, keeping time-to-market very short. While this can be a tremendous competitive advantage in today's business environment, it comes at a substantial cost. As applications become more mission-critical, and as desktop servers move into formal data centers, the number of servers in a data center grows, making the job of managing this disparate environment increasingly complex. Lower service levels and higher service level costs usually result from increased complexity. Remember, as complexity grows, so does the cost of managing it.

The organizational structures that are typically imposed on those who make the business decisions that affect data centers and those who manage data centers further add to this complexity. In most of the IT environments we deal with, multiple vertical entities control the budgets for developing applications and for funding the purchase of the servers to run them, while a single centralized IT operations group manages and maintains the applications and servers used by all of the vertical entities. This organization is found in nearly every industry including, but not limited to:

- Commercial companies: Business units, product lines, departments
- Government: Departments, agencies
- Military: Service, division, military base
- Academic: Department, professor, grant funds

In this type of environment, vertical entities have seemingly limitless freedom in how they develop and deploy applications and servers. Further, operations groups often have little or no control over the systems they manage or over the methods they use to manage them. For these reasons, it is very common for each application-server combination to be implemented and managed differently, and for a data center to lack the operational discipline found in most mainframe environments.

In these environments, IT operations staff tend to manage systems reactively. If something breaks, it gets fixed. They spend their time managing what has already happened rather than managing to prevent problems. Because of this, the IT operations people are the ones who feel the pain caused by this complexity, and they are usually the primary drivers of a consolidation project.

The following section explains the causes and effects of server sprawl on your data center.

Causes and Effects of Server Sprawl

The most frequent complaint we hear from Sun customers is that they have too many servers to manage, and that the problem is getting worse. Each new server adds complexity to their environments, and there is no relief in sight.

In the distributed computing environment, it is common for applications to be developed following a one-application-to-one-server model. Because funding for application development comes from vertical business units, and they insist on having their applications on their own servers, each time an application is put into production, another server is added. The problem created by this approach is significant because the one-application-to-one-server model is really a misnomer. In reality, each new application generally requires the addition of at least three new servers, and often requires more as follows:

- **Development servers.** The cardinal rule that you should not develop applications on the server you use for production creates a need for a separate development server for each new application. This guideline increases the number of servers required per application to two.

- **Test servers.** Once your application is coded, you need to test it before it goes into production. At a minimum, this requires you to unit test the application. If the application will interact with other applications, you must also perform integration testing. This action results in at least one, and possibly two, additional servers for the testing process. Because many developers insist on testing in an environment that is as close to the production environment as possible, this condition often results in large, fully configured test servers with large attached storage and databases. The server population has now grown to three or four servers.

- **Training servers.** If a new application will be used by lots of people, you may need to conduct training classes. This condition usually results in another server, so now we're up to four or five servers.

- **Multitier servers.** Many applications are developed using an n-tier architecture. In an n-tier architecture, various components of the application are separated and run on specialized servers; therefore, we frequently see a separate presentation tier, business tier, and resource tier. This architecture exacerbates server sprawl and adds to the complexity of the IT environment.

- **Cluster and disaster recovery servers.** If an application is deemed to be mission-critical, it may require a clustered environment, requiring one more server. If an application is extremely mission-critical, for example, like many of those in the financial district of New York City, it will require a disaster recovery site that allows for failover to the backup site. These requirements have the potential to add one or two more servers.

Now you can see how a single new application adds at least seven new servers to a data center. This configuration is why we see customers with several thousand servers.

To fully understand how this type of server sprawl adds complexity to a data center, you must also recognize that each time you add another server to your environment, you are also adding:

- Additional data storage that has to be managed and backed up
- Additional networking requirements
- Additional security requirements

Probably the largest impact of server sprawl is the complexity that results from the methods used to manage the environment. In many distributed computing environments, we find that there are as many different ways to manage servers as there are system administrators. This is where the lack of discipline found in data centers really stands out. If you can somehow take charge of this complexity, you can eliminate much of it, and simplify your job.

The following chapters explain how you can sell and implement a consolidation project as a method for reducing complexity and its negative effects.

Summary

This chapter provided a definition of consolidation, and explained how data centers have evolved to a point where consolidation has become necessary. In addition, it explained the causes and effects of complexity in today's IT environment. In general, with complexity comes increased costs, decreased service levels, and decreased availability. Consolidation seeks to reverse this trend. It is a movement towards higher service levels and lower service level costs. This goal is the reason consolidation has been a hot topic for several years, and it is the reason today's economic environment has accelerated the move to consolidate not just servers, but everything in the IT environment.

As we dig deeper into consolidation in the following chapters, it's important to remember that the reason for consolidation is really very simple:

- If you consolidate such that you reduce the number of devices you have to manage, and if you reduce the number of ways you manage them, you can reduce the complexity of your environment.
- If you reduce the complexity of your environment, you can increase the efficiency of your infrastructure.
- If you increase the efficiency of your infrastructure, you increase service levels and availability, and you lower your TCO.

Total cost of Ownership

## CHAPTER 2

Business Aspects of Consolidation

The decision to consolidate servers, or storage, is primarily a business decision. The technology considerations simply help you decide what you can and cannot consolidate. Before you begin any consolidation project, prove that there is a sufficient business need for it. If there isn't an obvious business justification, you probably shouldn't undertake it.

This chapter examines the business justifications for consolidation. It explains the importance of properly estimating the cost of complexity and understanding total cost of ownership (TCO), and provides recommendations for avoiding some of the common problems that can prevent a successful consolidation. Topics presented in this chapter include:

- "Establishing a Business Justification for Consolidation" on page 9
- "Estimating the Cost of Complexity" on page 12
- "Understanding Total Cost of Ownership" on page 13
- "Avoiding Common Pitfalls and Failures" on page 19

Establishing a Business Justification for Consolidation

When we talk with chief information officers (CIOs) about the major business problems they face, their primary reasons for considering data center consolidation include a desire to accomplish the following goals:

- Reduce TCO.
- Improve service levels.
- Provide increased application availability.
- Increase the manageability of the information technology (IT) environment.

While the potential to reduce TCO is one of the most effective business drivers for consolidation, combining reduced TCO with a considerable return on investment (ROI) makes consolidation a very attractive solution, not just to CIOs, but also to the other CxOs (Chief Executive Officer [CEO], Chief Financial Officer [CFO], and the like).

Just as business issues can drive consolidation, they can also hinder or prevent it. Consolidation may be the chicken soup for the data center's ills, but you have to get the patient to eat it for it to work. Think of establishing a clear business justification as the diagnosis of your patient's condition. It is the first step towards healing your patient.

In Chapter 1, we looked at some of the historical and technical reasons for consolidation; now let's take a look at some of the business justifications for it. When you provide a business justification to the executives who must approve it, consider how your business can benefit from improvements in the following categories:

- Reducing IT costs
- Keeping up with business challenges
- Improving service levels and availability
- Minimizing the impact of external pressures

Reducing IT Costs

There is a definite sentiment in today's corporate environment that IT costs are too high, and need to be reduced. We see this in virtually every account we visit. However, there are several trends in IT that continue to drive costs higher. The following paragraphs explain how consolidation can help you reduce costs associated with complexity, staffing, and building.

Reduce Costs Associated With Complexity

A major benefit of consolidation is the ability to use it to decrease costs associated with complexity in today's IT environments. In Chapter 1, we explained the extent to which server sprawl contributes to increased complexity and increased costs. Another factor that contributes to complexity, and therefore contributes to increased costs, is the change in development models for application architectures from monolithic to n-tier.

Developers used to create applications as a single large program or group of programs that ran on a single server. The demands of web-based and e-commerce applications have changed this application model. In today's development world, it is common to find applications broken into tiers, where each tier has a specific purpose and focus. Consider, for example, a three-tier application with web or content servers, application servers, and a database server. In this model, the one-application-to-one-server model has been changed to one application with many layers running on many servers.

To reduce the complexity-associated costs that result from server sprawl and tiered applications, consolidate the methods you use to manage these servers. Remember, there are many ways to reduce complexity. While a certain amount of system complexity is unavoidable, you can almost always minimize the processes you use to manage it.

Reduce Staffing Costs

One of the biggest benefits of consolidating your environment is that it enables you to control people costs. In every major city that we visit, there is a shortage of talented system administrators, database administrators (DBAs), and network specialists. When you can find the right people, they are very expensive. By consolidating your environment, you can make a more efficient use of resources, and minimize the impact of staffing costs on your budget.

Reduce Building Costs

The high cost of setting up computer rooms is another major expense. As servers proliferate, they take up more and more of the available data center floor space. This is a major concern because computer rooms are very expensive to build. Typical costs for raised floor computer rooms in the Silicon Valley area are in the neighborhood of $500 per square foot. In New York City, this increases to around $1000 per square foot. Consolidation can help reduce the need for new computer rooms by making more efficient use of existing facilities. Although this doesn't necessarily reduce the ongoing cost of operations, it definitely helps avoid a major capital expenditure.

Keeping Up With Business Challenges

The demands on today's businesses to stay competitive and to provide faster times-to-market are ever growing. If you fail to take advantage of business opportunities in a timely fashion, you risk being at a competitive disadvantage. Companies grow through increased sales, as well as through acquisitions and mergers. As new business opportunities are explored, new technologies are often deployed. All of this growth increases the complexity and the cost of IT environments. By consolidating your environment and the methods you use to manage them, you can improve your ability to manage this complexity, and to quickly and effectively respond to these challenges.

Improving Service Levels and Availability

As you consolidate within the data center, it becomes easier to manage the never-ending cycle of day-to-day tasks such as upgrades, patches, reconfigurations, fixes, balancing workloads, and backups. Consolidation motivates IT organizations to standardize and centralize systems and management practices. This standardization, in turn, enables you to manage IT environments more efficiently. With increased efficiency come higher service levels, higher availability, and lower costs.

High service levels and availability generally translate into increased revenues and decreased costs. Because of this, we are now starting to see much more interest in consolidation from the vertical business units who formerly opposed consolidation.

Minimizing the Impact of External Pressures

There are a variety of pressures external to IT operations that contribute to the need to consolidate. As vertical business units develop, their servers are managed part time, and often ineffectively, by developers who do not have those management functions as part of their job descriptions. This situation often causes end-user frustration, and can negatively affect end-user productivity levels. By placing servers into the controlled environment of the data center, where they are subject to consolidation and more structured management practices, you can minimize the impact of external pressures on your data center.

Estimating the Cost of Complexity

In "Complexity in the Data Center" on page 6, we explained how complexity affects the data center. Primarily, we noted that increased complexity results in decreased efficiency and increased TCO. While the cost of this complexity is difficult to measure, estimating it provides you with information to prove that a consolidation is needed, and to justify the investment it requires. This section provides recommendations for estimating the cost of complexity in your data center.

Sun's internal IT operations group developed the following graph to quantify the cost of managing increasingly complex environments. The basic premise is that the greater the number of different platforms you have to manage, the more expensive it becomes to manage with the same service levels on a per platform basis. This relationship clearly shows that managing fewer different platforms is much less complex and much more cost efficient than managing multiple different platforms.

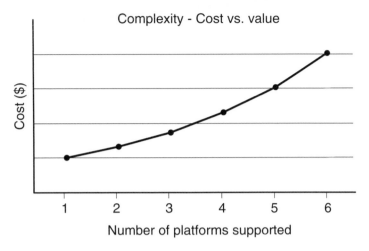

FIGURE 2-1 Cost of Managing Complex Environments

While this chart was developed to demonstrate the cost of complexity in the server environment, we argue that the concept it illustrates can be extended to other IT environments, such as storage and middleware.

Several major analyst groups have published papers within the last 18 months that support the point illustrated in the preceding graphic. They agree that reducing the complexity of IT environments can help drive down TCO and increase manageability. For example, one analyst group estimated that for each variant of an operating system (OS), such as UNIX, you add to your environment, you should expect a 25 percent decrease in the number of servers that can be effectively managed by a single system administrator. This statement is even more pessimistic than our chart forecasts.

As you look at the complexity caused by server sprawl and at the cost generated by it, you can see why an increasing number of companies are interested in consolidating their IT environments. The following chapter provides information about the specific consolidation opportunities that exist.

Understanding Total Cost of Ownership

TCO is a much talked-about topic; virtually everyone wants to reduce it. Understanding TCO is critical to identify potential ROI, as well as to measure the success of a project once it is completed. To know if you have reduced your costs as a result of a consolidation project, you must measure TCO before the project, perform the consolidation, and then, six months to a year later, remeasure your TCO. Only then, can you determine the true value of the consolidated solution. This sounds simple, but it's not.

One of the biggest difficulties in measuring TCO is defining what it means to you. If you sit down at a table with 10 CIOs and ask each of them to define TCO, you will likely get 10 very different answers. In our experience, very few businesses have a clear definition of TCO. When we find companies that have defined what TCO means to them, their definition is often complex and difficult to measure.

When you look to outside consulting groups for TCO models, you find a variety of proposed solutions. Sometimes they are called TCO, and sometimes they are called something else. Some of the different models we have found include:

- **Total cost of ownership (TCO).** A concept largely developed by Gartner over the last few years, TCO is the methodology used by Sun Professional Services. It focuses on the costs of an IT environment.

- **Total economic impact (TEI).** Developed by Giga Information Group, TEI focuses on how a solution or initiative impacts not only IT but the company's business units as well.

- **Total value of ownership (TVO).** Developed by Lucidus Ltd. in the UK, TVO focuses not only on the costs of ownership of IT assets, but also on the value those assets bring to the corporation.

There are probably several other models, but it doesn't matter which model you use as long as you agree with the model's basic concepts and as long as it yields the desired results. In our case, we use Gartner's TCO model.

Following an Established TCO Methodology

When we started to focus on consolidation in 1997, we wanted to find a TCO methodology that already existed and was accepted by our customers. During an internal Sun class, we discovered that a former Sun IT finance director was working on TCO concepts at SunLabs, Sun's internal think tank. After much research, she discovered that Gartner had a TCO model that seemed to make a lot of sense. She validated it with outside consultants who were knowledgeable in the area, and decided to adopt the Gartner model. Because we didn't want to reinvent the wheel, and since she was much more capable of evaluating various TCO models than we were, we accepted her recommendation.

Gartner was probably the first analyst group to really explore the concept of TCO, and what it meant to IT. In many circles, Bill Kirwin, a Gartner analyst, is regarded as the father of TCO. In addition, Gartner also offers software packages that allow you to measure TCO, and to perform TCO simulations using their methodology.

One of the greatest benefits of using Gartner's TCO methodology and software is that they provide and support a credible, third-party definition of TCO. By using their methodology, we can't be accused of slanting the numbers and recommendations in Sun's favor.

Gartner's Definition of TCO

Gartner defines TCO as the costs associated with an asset throughout the entire life cycle of the asset; it is not just the cost of the hardware. TCO includes the cost of acquisition, deployment, ongoing management, and even the retirement of the asset. Many companies mistakenly look only at the acquisition cost of servers or storage. Most analysts agree that the acquisition cost, or capital cost, of an asset represents only a small part of the TCO for that asset. Depending on which analyst you talk with, the acquisition cost represents only 5–30 percent of TCO. The number we usually use for acquisition cost is around 15 percent of TCO. The rest is comprised of the various ongoing costs of running and managing the asset.

The Gartner TCO model utilizes two major categories to organize costs: direct costs and indirect costs.

- **Direct (budgeted) costs.** These costs are the capital, fees, and labor costs spent by the corporate IT department, business units, and departmental IT groups to deliver IT services and solutions to the organization and users. Costs include hardware and software expenses, information systems operations labor, service desk labor, information systems finance and administration labor, outsourced management, and support fees. Direct costs model typical costs, and capture actual costs for all expenses related to clients (mobile and desktop), servers, peripherals, and networks in the distributed computing environment and serving distributed computing users.

- **Indirect (unbudgeted) costs.** These costs measure the efficiency of the IT group to deliver expected services to end users. If the IT management and solutions are efficient, end users are less likely to be burdened with self and peer support, as well as downtime. If the IT management and solutions are inefficient, end users typically spend more time supporting themselves and each other (self and peer support), and are impacted by more downtime.

  In most organizations, indirect costs are hidden and are not measured or tracked. Because of this, many organizations undertake direct cost reduction programs, but can unknowingly transfer the burden of support and unreliability to end users.

Gartner research has shown that inefficient or overly aggressive spending cuts can lead to $4 in lost productivity for every $1 saved. You can view indirect costs as a second-order effect that IT spending, or lack thereof, has on the organization. It cannot be measured directly, and there is not always a direct causal relationship.

Efficient IT spending can have a direct positive impact on end-user productivity, while inefficient spending or cuts can cost an organization more in lost productivity than was saved in spending cuts.

The following graphic shows the various cost elements in the Gartner chart of accounts for TCO.

DIRECT			INDIRECT
Capital	**Labor**	**Fees/Other**	
Hardware	**Management**	**Communication**	**End user IS**
Servers	Network	WAN	Peer/self support
Clients	System	Service provider	Casual learning
Peripherals	Storage	RAS	Scripting/
Network	**Support**	Internet access	development
Software	Executive and	provider	End-user
Operating	administration	Client access	Training
systems	Help desk	**Management and**	Satisfaction
Applications	Training	**Support**	**Downtime**
Utilities	Procurement	Outsourcing	Planned
IS	**Development**	Maintenance	Unplanned
Acquisition	Infrastructure	contracts	
costs	Business	Support contracts	
Depreciation	applications	Service levels	
Leasing		performance and	
Expense		service level	
Upgrades and		metrics	
supplies			

FIGURE 2-2   Gartner Chart of Accounts—Reasons for Measuring TCO

Gartner TCO Software

Gartner offers a variety of software packages to support various types of TCO. The software we use focuses on the distributed computing environment and on storage. We normally use Gartner TCO Analyst software to perform TCO simulations as part of a consolidation; however, another version of the software, Gartner TCO Manager, is also available. Both packages let you perform TCO simulations, but TCO Manager also lets you collect actual TCO data and generate TCO reports (activities we generally do not perform because simulation provides us with the information we need in a much shorter time frame).

Simulate TCO

When we analyze potential TCO savings, we almost always focus on TCO simulations. Actual TCO measurement engagements are time consuming and costly. If accurate data is available, a TCO measurement will usually last 8–12 weeks and will require 100–200 hours of consulting time and 300–400 hours of client time.

A TCO simulation, on the other hand, is a relatively quick, low-cost method of obtaining TCO and ROI information. When we perform a TCO simulation as part of a feasibility study, it usually takes one week (or less) to complete. In our experience, TCO simulation performed using Gartner software generally produces results with an accuracy of plus or minus 10 percent, which is good enough for most consolidation projects.

When you perform a TCO simulation, you gather information about the IT configuration and use it as input to the Gartner software. Gartner TCO Analyst uses an internal database, the Gartner TCO Index, to estimate TCO for the configuration. The TCO Index is based on over 1000 actual Gartner TCO measurements. The index takes into account the geographic location of the client, the size of the business, and the business type. The resulting report is an estimate of the TCO that Gartner would expect to find for this client if they performed an actual TCO measurement.

Sample TCO Simulation

The simulation in this sample was performed for a large petroleum company in the Southwestern U.S. The data center we analyzed had approximately 500 servers. The client was interested in a server consolidation project for this data center, and wanted us to estimate the potential TCO savings for reducing the number of servers by one-third, by half, and by two-thirds.

Not surprisingly, the TCO savings increased as the number of servers decreased. For a two-thirds reduction in the number of servers, Gartner TCO Analyst showed that there was a potential savings of approximately $14 million and a TCO reduction of over 50 percent. This relationship is shown in the following bar graph, which was generated by TCO Analyst.

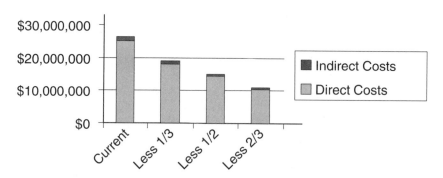

TCO Analysis Overview - Server Only

FIGURE 2-3 Increased TCO Savings With Decreased Number of Servers

We estimated that a project to consolidate two-thirds of the client's servers would cost around $12 million. The projected TCO savings over a three-year period was about $40 million. This meant that a break-even point would be reached in 15–18 months, and the net positive cash flow over the three-year period would be about $28 million, as shown in the following line chart generated by TCO Analyst. These numbers provided the client with plenty of justification for the consolidation project.

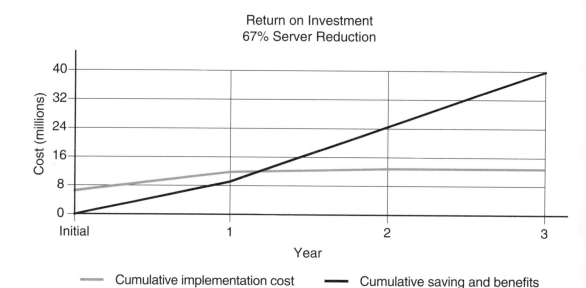

FIGURE 2-4 Return on Investment of $28 Million After Three Years

Avoiding Common Pitfalls and Failures

Consolidation projects can provide enormous benefits when they are completed successfully, but there are several things that can derail or hinder a consolidation project. This section describes some of these common pitfalls and failures, and explains how you can use the following tasks to avoid them:

- Convince business units to surrender servers.
- Gain and maintain executive sponsorship.
- Manage politics.
- Apply best practices and adhere to standards.
- Develop and adhere to well-defined processes.
- Rely on established consolidation methodologies.
- Consider prohibitive bandwidth costs of high data-traffic applications.
- Select appropriate applications to consolidate together.
- Identify application or middleware coexistence problems.
- Consider legal requirements to keep data locally.

Convincing Business Units to Surrender Their Servers

Individual business units usually own the budget that pays for developing new applications and purchasing the servers and storage that will run the new applications. Because of this, they usually resist any efforts by the IT group to run their applications on a server with other applications. They don't want the risk having another application affect theirs. This can be an extremely difficult issue to deal with, and we cannot state strongly enough that these political issues must be dealt with, or an application consolidation will not get off the ground.

At Sun, we have been urging customers to combine applications on large servers, such as the Sun Enterprise™ 10000 and Sun Fire™ 15K, for several years. We have had a strong focus on providing services to applications, not just providing servers to applications.

There are a variety of techniques that you can use to ensure that applications can successfully share a single instance of the Solaris Operating Environment. If you can show a business unit that their fears are unfounded, you can usually persuade them to go along with consolidation plans.

Gaining and Maintaining Executive Sponsorship

IT operations groups often sponsor consolidation projects. They understand the issues of managing complexity, and they want to make situations better for themselves and for the corporations where they work. The only way for operations to drive a consolidation project is to obtain executive sponsorship at the highest possible levels. We recommend that this sponsorship be at least at the vice president or director level. If you get executive sponsorship, it is much easier to sell consolidation down to the lower levels of the business unit. Conversely, if you sell consolidation at the lower levels and expect it to float to the top, you will usually be disappointed.

Further, it is critical that you gain sponsorship in IT management, as well as vertical business unit management. If high-level executive sponsorship is not present to help drive consolidation down through the ranks, the consolidation project will likely fail.

Just as it is important to gain executive buy-in for the concept of consolidation early on, it is also important to continue to sell consolidation throughout the project. Once you gain executive sponsorship, you must continually maintain it. Keep your sponsor actively involved before, during, and after the consolidation project. If you don't, you may find that although your project was technically sound, you may not have achieved the desired business results. Remember that successful consolidation projects can have substantial business benefits. If you have the right executive sponsorship and you are successful, that success also reflects positively on your sponsor.

Managing Politics

By far, the most prevalent inhibitor to consolidation is internal politics. Once you've gained executive sponsorship, you must socialize that support throughout the affected business units. Often, vertical business units don't trust consolidation and don't want you to tamper with their applications. Unless this objection is overcome, consolidation projects are doomed to failure.

There are two ways to approach overcoming these challenges. We refer to this as a carrot-and-stick strategy. The carrot approach would be to demonstrate to the business unit that consolidation is an attractive option that can help deliver improved service levels and reduced TCO. The stick approach is for IT operations to take over ownership of the IT assets and control them directly. This doesn't have to be an either-or solution; you may find an optimal solution lies somewhere in between.

Applying Best Practices and Adhering to Standards

We often find that our clients do not have well-developed standards in a variety of areas. Consistently using best practices and adhering to established standards can greatly improve your ability to provide high service levels to your customers, while at the same time lowering TCO. When you model the implementation of standards using the Gartner TCO Analyst software, you will find that the potential TCO savings are often 10–20 percent.

Application development standards are another area that can make or break a consolidation. If developers are allowed to write applications any way they want, they often produce software that is not friendly to other applications. If you establish and impose development standards that specify how developers write applications, it is easy to control these adverse practices. For example, you might require that developers access OS features through vendor approved application programming interfaces. Doing so can decrease the chance of application failures that may affect other applications in a consolidated environment.

Developing and Adhering to Well-Defined Processes

The development and application of well-defined processes are critical to the successful operation of a data center. If you don't have them in place in your data center before you begin a consolidation, you must put them in place during the consolidation project. If you don't, you may greatly increase the risk of failures in the consolidated environment.

As you develop processes and procedures for the data center, it is important to keep in mind that you don't want to re-create the rigid and inflexible processes that caused staff to rebel against the mainframe environment in the first place. You need to strike a happy medium between control and flexibility.

Sun Professional Services offers a service called the Sun Ready[SM] Availability Assessment (SRAA) to assess the ability of a customer's IT infrastructure and organization to sustain appropriate access, performance, function, and service levels within the limits and expectations defined by the customer and their end users. This service can be applied to a specific environment, or to a business application. In addition, it's designed to identify gaps in a customer's technical architecture and operational infrastructure that may affect availability. Also, the SRAA identifies gaps that may affect the customer's ability to meet the service level commitments the customer has made (implicitly and explicitly) to its end users.

Based on these evaluations, this report makes recommendations for improving availability in each of the following 10 IT infrastructure areas:

- Service management
- Account management
- Program management
- Staff management
- Asset management
- Problem management
- Implementation management
- Change management
- Execution management
- Improvement management

If you are unsure of your data center processes, a third-party assessment, such as the SRAA, can be an invaluable part of your consolidation project.

Relying on Established Consolidation Methodologies

If you have never done a consolidation, working with someone who performs them often may be very valuable. If you are going to hire a third party to work with you, make sure they have the right people for your project and that they have a complete methodology. Ask for references, and make sure they have proof of successful consolidation engagements.

Considering Prohibitive Bandwidth Costs of High Data-Traffic Applications

In many parts of the world, our customers are trying to drastically reduce the number of data centers they support. When you consolidate data centers, you may run into major network bandwidth problems. You have to be able to support the aggregate bandwidth requirements of your applications. If the proper network bandwidth is not readily available, obtaining it may be prohibitively expensive. If this is the case, it may be difficult to financially justify a consolidation.

There may also be technical prohibitions to consolidating data centers. Many applications, especially online transaction processing (OLTP) applications like Oracle Financials or SAP, may not tolerate significant latency that can be introduced by wide area networking. It may lead to problems with both your user population productivity and possibly the performance of the application. This problem can be magnified by the fact that many data center consolidations will be over vast distances, to ensure lower physical and operational costs.

Selecting Appropriate Applications to Consolidate Together

In the mainframe world, immature partitioning and immature workload management capabilities are not an issue. Mainframes handle the workload management issues for a variety of applications and protect applications from each other. In the open-systems world, however, workload management is still immature when compared to the mainframe. This means that you have to be careful when you select applications to consolidate together.

The lack of mainframe-type workload management does not have to be a hindrance. We have worked with many companies who do not use any workload management software in their projects. When they consolidate, they don't push the limits of the server. Instead of trying for 60–70 percent utilization on the consolidated server, they settle for much lower utilization (for example, 40–50 percent). If you want to shoot for 70 percent utilization, the workload management capabilities of the Solaris Operating Environment can provide an extra level of protection. They can help manage your applications and ensure that they get adequate resources in the consolidated environment. Information about resource management is provided in Chapter 8, "Designing a Consolidated Architecture."

Identifying Application or Middleware Coexistence Problems

If you are running mostly purchased, third-party applications from independent software vendors (ISVs), your consolidation opportunities may be limited. These vendors often specify that no other applications can be resident on a server that is running their software. The penalty for violating this policy is that the ISV usually refuses to support their application.

Some ISV software is simply consolidation unfriendly. Applications may do things such as locking up a particular resource and making it unavailable to other applications. For example, some supply chain software tries to lock up all available memory on a server. This is obviously behavior that does not lend itself to consolidation.

Considering Legal Requirements to Keep Data Locally

In some countries, there are laws that dictate if and how data can be transmitted across the country's borders. If you are doing business in one of these countries, you may find that these laws prevent you from consolidating some applications. For example, in Japan, the banking and finance industry that regulates the trading and storage of certain commodities requires that treasury data to remain in the country. Other examples include privacy protection laws in Europe that prevent the transmission of data across various countries' borders.

Summary

In this chapter, we explained the business issues to consider when preparing for a consolidation project. This chapter provided guidance for selling a consolidation project to management, provided methods for properly assessing the cost of complexity and TCO, and explained how to avoid some of the problems you may face during a consolidation project.

## CHAPTER 3

Types of Consolidation

When we started working on consolidation four years ago, the focus was on server consolidation; now, the emphasis has changed. When you walk into a data center and look around, everything you see is a candidate for consolidation. Today, consolidation is about reducing the number of devices you have to manage, and reducing the number of ways you use to manage them.

With that in mind, let's take a look at some of the consolidation opportunities that exist in today's information technology (IT) environment. These include:

Consolidating Servers

Servers are still the primary focal point for consolidation because they are so obvious. Whether you have 100 servers or 5000 servers, you probably have too many to manage effectively. Today's distributed computing environment lends itself to a proliferation of servers. Reducing and controlling the number of devices to manage, and simplifying ways to manage them are the goals of most IT groups.

Applying Vertical and Horizontal Scalability

When we talk about consolidating servers, we generally refer to scaling them vertically or horizontally.

- Vertical scalability enables you to reduce the number of servers by consolidating multiple applications onto a single server.

- Horizontal scalability enables you to deal with increased workloads through the replication of servers, and the distribution of workloads across those servers.

By thinking of consolidation in these terms, you begin to define the approach required by your particular consolidation project. Once you decide whether your consolidation project requires horizontal scaling, vertical scaling, or a combination of the two, you can further refine your approach by identifying patterns in your server population. Examples of vertical and horizontal scaling are presented in Chapter 8.

Identifying Patterns in an End-to-End Architecture

In the end-to-end architectures that are prevalent today, tiers of servers are specialized for particular tasks. When you look at consolidating servers, you need to look for patterns in your server population. When you identify these patterns within tiers, you can start to devise a consolidation strategy. Scalability is the key, here. Because you are expected to deliver predictable service levels in response to unpredictable workloads, it is important that you use the right type of scalability for each part of a consolidated architecture. The following sections describe common patterns in an end-to-end architecture.

For consolidation discussions, we generally assume that there are three server types, or tiers:

- The presentation tier is the closest tier to the end user.

- The business, or middleware, tier is where applications or middleware run in conjunction with the other tiers.

- The resource tier is where large, scalable servers run mission-critical applications and databases.

Although architectures with these characteristics have been around for awhile, most corporations still have many servers running monolithic applications. In many cases, these are older servers running mature applications. These servers are generally excellent candidates for server and application consolidation.

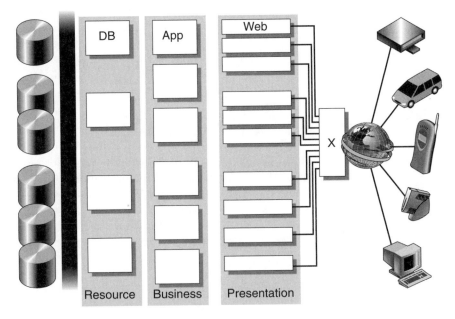

FIGURE 3-1 End-to-End Architecture

Presentation Tier

As you get closer to the Internet and the delivery devices for your applications, the most common techniques for scalability are replication and load balancing across an array of generally small servers. This process is usually referred to as horizontal scalability.

On the presentation tier, you usually find several small, one or two processor servers running UNIX, Linux, or Microsoft Windows. Because current architectures call for many small servers in this tier, the opportunities for consolidating to fewer servers are limited. Despite these limitations, there is still ample opportunity to implement standards and best practices to simplify the management of these servers, and to reduce total cost of ownership (TCO).

Business Tier

After the presentation tier, you find business-tier servers. These servers generally run applications or middleware in conjunction with the other tiers. While we used to see primarily horizontal scaling in this tier, there is growing interest in reducing the number of applications using vertical scalability, as well.

Resource Tier

The resource tier is usually thought of as the heart of the data center. It is characterized by large, scalable servers that run mission-critical applications and databases. We usually find the most interest in vertical scalability and server consolidation on this tier.

Identifying Types of Consolidation

Some major consulting groups identify different categories of server consolidation. For example, Gartner refers to physical, logical, and rational consolidation groups—categories we define in the following sections. The techniques used to achieve these specific types of consolidations are discussed in later chapters.

Physical Consolidation

Physical consolidation involves consolidating data centers and moving servers to fewer physical locations. The theory behind physical consolidation is that by having servers in fewer physical locations, you can achieve management consistencies and economies of scale more easily than you can when your servers are dispersed. Physical consolidations may also enable you to reduce data center real estate costs. It is generally felt that physical consolidation has the lowest risk, but that it also has the lowest payback.

Logical Consolidation

Logical consolidation involves implementing standards and best practices across your server population. By doing this, you can realize substantial benefits in the productivity of your IT staff. They can manage the environment more efficiently and more effectively. This improvement can often result in lower systems management costs and in lower TCO. Logical consolidation is often implemented with physical consolidation and rationalization.

Rationalization

Rationalization involves the deployment of multiple applications on fewer, larger servers and in fewer instances of the operating system (OS). Because TCO reduction is closely tied to the number of instances of an OS you manage, reducing the number is the best way to reduce TCO. While rationalization is the riskiest form of server consolidation, it offers the biggest TCO reduction and return on investment (ROI).

Because of its potential to reduce TCO and increase ROI, we find that most of our customers find rationalization to be the most attractive method for consolidation, despite its higher risks. During a recent web seminar on consolidation, we polled over 300 attendees on whether their main interest was in physical consolidation, logical consolidation, or rationalization. Over 85 percent said their primary interest was in rationalization.

dating Applications

ch server resources applications use and understanding usage
l to the process of consolidating servers. This process is
the chapters about assessment and architecture.

k about consolidation, people always ask which applications
consolidate. There is no easy answer to this question, and
application individually. The people who know the
velopers, database administrators, and system
are of them on a daily basis. Talking with these people
d and bad consolidation candidates rather quickly.

Eliminating Consolidation Candidates

While it is not easy to make specific recommendations about which applications are good consolidation candidates, there are some general guidelines you can follow to eliminate candidates from consolidation.

First and foremost, consider eliminating all servers and storage that are deliberately isolated from other servers. This includes:

- Firewalls
- Intrusions detection servers
- Sensitive databases
- Geographically separated servers

Isolation and separation are vital attributes of many security-related servers. Unless you are specifically targeting these machines, they are probably too complex to consolidate without a complete reevaluation of the security architecture. After you have consolidated the rest of your environment, you can come back and look for opportunities for security consolidations. The same is true for servers or storage that are geographically separated. For instance, if you have separated servers for redundancy or wide area network (WAN) reasons, it hardly makes sense to try to consolidate these together.

Third-party applications developed and sold by independent software vendors (ISVs) may be problematic as consolidation candidates. In many cases, ISVs specify that their applications run in standalone mode on their own servers. If this is not done, they usually do not provide support for the application. Make sure you check with your vendors for their support requirements.

Other applications that do not qualify for consolidation include those that lock up system resources, such as physical memory. If you aren't sure about an application's suitability for consolidation in this respect, make sure you analyze it with a performance tool such as TeamQuest or BMC's Patrol-Perform and Predict.

Applying Backward and Forward Consolidation Strategies

When most people begin their consolidation efforts, they often focus on existing applications. This process is known as a backward consolidation. In many cases, these consolidations are hugely successful. In others, organizational issues prevent them from achieving their goals. There is no doubt that some of the largest and most successful consolidations we have seen have been backward consolidations.

To avoid future server sprawl, it is also important to begin to develop new applications in a consolidated environment, referred to as forward consolidation. It's interesting to note that applications that are developed in a consolidated environment usually behave with each other, and can be moved into production in a consolidated environment.

Consolidating Application Sets

When you analyze a group of servers for consolidation, it is important to identify the applications that run on them. It is equally important to identify the servers and applications with which the consolidation candidates interact. It's very common to find groups of applications that receive data from other applications or that supply data to other applications. Because these applications process information sequentially, they are often excellent candidates for consolidation. These application sets don't usually compete for the same resources at the same time, and when you group them within a single instance of the OS, you often find that they perform better because of intradomain communications. A decrease in network traffic is often a side benefit of consolidating application sets.

When deciding which application sets to consolidate, we generally categorize them as being tightly coupled or loosely coupled. In tightly coupled application sets, applications actively interact with each other. In loosely coupled sets, a group of applications acquire and process data, and then pass them on to the next server.

As an example of a successful consolidation of tightly coupled applications, consider a situation where a customer gathered home-grown enterprise resource planning applications, Tuxedo messaging, and an Oracle database server, and moved them into a single instance of the OS. The results were extremely successful. Application throughput increased, and network usage decreased. From a scalability viewpoint, the transaction volume of the application set increased from roughly 40,000 sales order lines per day, two years ago, to over 400,000 sales order lines per day. This was obviously a successful consolidation, and a successful application of vertical scalability.

As an example of a loosely coupled application set, consider a situation where a server runs an online transaction processing (OLTP) application during the day, then at night, passes the transaction information to a batch server for further processing and reporting. The batch server would then update a data warehouse server, which would, in turn, update multiple data mart servers. Each server depends on another, but not simultaneously.

Consolidating Multiple Database Instances

A very common example of server and application consolidation is to put multiple instances of a database in a single instance of the OS. This is a very common tactic with most major databases. It's important to note that you don't want to mix these two databases on the same instance of the OS; doing so may cause fatal application conflicts.

The success of this consolidation strategy depends heavily on development standards and practices. Where strict naming conventions are followed and each instance of the database is unique, consolidations are successful. However, on an occasion when we worked with a customer who wrote multiple Oracle applications and chose to use default naming conventions, multiple conflicts resulted between database instances. Obviously, this consolidation was not successful.

Consolidating Similar Workloads

Another consolidation technique that some consultants recommend is to consolidate similar workloads with like resource usage and time scheduling. If you do this, you need to understand the application's resource usage very clearly. When using this consolidation technique, the key to success is that you must offset the timing of resource usage for each workload. Otherwise, you simply end up with overlapping peaks and valleys of resource usage.

Consolidating Storage

Today, there is as much interest in storage consolidation as there is in server consolidation. As we said earlier, every new server you deploy results in more storage. In many cases, the cost of storage for a server exceeds the cost of the server, and although the server may not grow very much, the amount of storage required for an application will grow indefinitely.

When you look at application sets, you find a lot of data replication because multiple applications look at the same data. For example, if you have an OLTP server, a batch server, a data warehouse server, and four data mart servers, you may have seven copies of a particular dataset such as a customer master file. While, in theory, all seven copies are identical, because different developers probably created their applications, it is likely that there will be differences in each copy of the data. This situation has the potential to create a situation where reports run on the "same" data, yet yield different results.

As with servers, the goals in storage consolidation are to reduce complexity, increase utilization, and reduce TCO. These goals can be achieved through a variety of consolidation techniques. The ultimate goal is data sharing among applications. Unfortunately, this often requires redesigning and redeveloping applications, so it is a long-term goal, at least for backward consolidation. In a forward consolidation, data sharing should absolutely be a goal.

Other benefits of storage consolidation include:

- Easier backup and recovery
- Increased availability
- Improved scalability
- Storage resource pooling

When undertaking a storage consolidation effort, it is critical that you understand how disk space is utilized. While most of our customers can't tell us exactly what their current disk space utilization rates are, many companies we have surveyed estimate a rate of 40 percent, or less. For companies that have tried to accurately assess disk utilization, complexity often hinders their efforts. For example, one company we visited started counting storage, but stopped at 110 terabytes after realizing that they just couldn't count it all. When we evaluated their disk utilization, we found they were utilizing only 20 percent of their available storage.

There are several types of storage consolidation available today. The following sections describe the three most common types we see.

Consolidating Servers and Their Associated Storage

With every server consolidation, there is an accompanying storage consolidation. As you move multiple applications to a single instance of the OS, you must also move their storage, as shown in the following graphic. In theory, once you have moved the storage, data will be available to any of the applications. This situation is the most primitive form of storage consolidation.

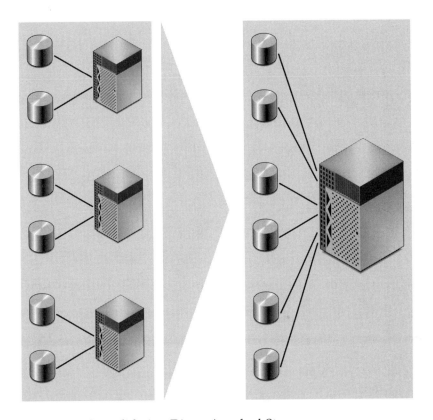

FIGURE 3-2 Consolidating Direct-Attached Storage

Connecting Heterogeneous Environments to a Single Storage Component

Many of our customers have heterogeneous IT environments. They run servers and OSs from many vendors, and they want to access data from a variety of different servers. With direct-attached storage, this was difficult to do. Now, with products like the Sun StorEdge™ 9900 storage array, it is possible to connect the Solaris Operating Environment servers, other UNIX servers, Windows NT servers, and mainframe servers to the same storage array. The following graphic demonstrates this capability.

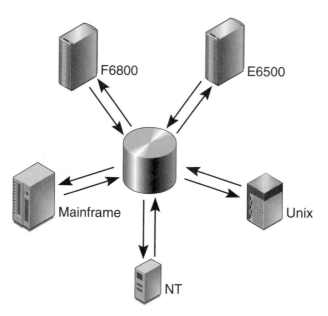

FIGURE 3-3   Heterogeneous Environments to Single Storage

This is a very popular type of storage consolidation, especially where there are multiple mission-critical applications running on servers from a variety of vendors.

Consolidating With Storage Area Networks

Storage area networks (SANs) have been the hottest trend in storage architectures for the last few years. As a technology, the SAN is now mature enough that it can be implemented using standards and standard configurations. As shown in the following graphic, SAN technology inserts a network, or fabric, of switching devices between servers and storage that enables any server or application to access any storage connected to it. The fabric can then be configured to allow various servers to access various storage.

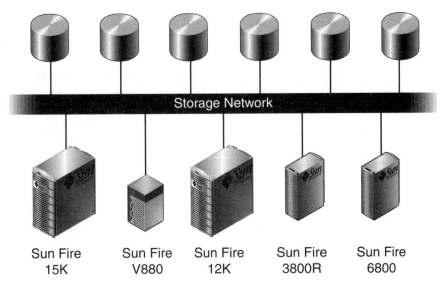

FIGURE 3-4 Storage Area Network (SAN) Configuration

Another hot storage technology is network attached storage (NAS). This technology allows servers and clients to utilize storage directly over the network using common networking protocols like network file system (NFS) and Server Message Block (SMB). Although not used greatly in many server and application consolidations within the data center, it is used extensively in file and print consolidations at the department and workgroup level. As the technology matures, expect it to work itself into data center consolidations.

Consolidating Shared Services

Another type of consolidation that is rapidly gaining popularity is middleware or shared services consolidation. Over the last few years, companies have implemented shared services (such as file, print, authentication, and email) in a variety of ways. Business units typically implement their own versions of these services using software from a variety of vendors. However, when they want to share some of this information, they find that the inconsistencies and incompatibilities among these various architectures increase complexity; thereby increasing cost and making it difficult to share. As a result, we often find that companies want to rebuild their shared services as web services using a standards-based, unified architecture such as Sun™ Open Net Environment (Sun ONE).

A common example of this is the use of directory services. Directory services have been implemented over the years using a variety of architectures. Now that standards-based architectures are available, products like the Sun ONE Directory Server, which is based on the Lightweight Directory Access Protocol (LDAP), are being used to design and implement corporate-wide directory services. Condensing multiple, disparate directory architectures into a single, corporate architecture allows corporations to simplify directory maintenance and easily replicate directory services, as needed.

We expect to see more of this type of consolidation over the next few years.

Consolidating Networks

When you consolidate servers and applications, network consolidation is usually either a big issue or not an issue at all. When you collapse data centers and concentrate servers and applications into fewer physical locations, there may be a severe impact on the network. This impact must be evaluated as part of the consolidation project. You certainly need to ensure that there is sufficient network bandwidth to handle network traffic to and from the consolidated location.

Conversely, when you do a rationalization within a single data center, you often find that there are no major network changes that need to take place. The overall traffic does not increase, because new servers and applications are not being introduced. Further, rationalization may actually decrease network traffic, because applications in a single instance of the OS don't need the network to communicate with each other.

Consolidating Data Centers

Many organizations are looking to consolidate multiple data centers into one site. These consolidations range from simple city-wide consolidations to complex region-wide consolidations. Most companies are being driven toward data center consolidation because of the dramatic drop in the cost of telecommunication wide area network lines, the huge disparity of IT wages between certain regions of the world, and the high real estate costs of large cities (especially in New York, London, and Tokyo). For those considering simple local-site consolidations, consolidation offers cost savings and enables disaster recovery initiatives.

If your organization is seriously looking to consolidate a data center, carefully consider the goals for consolidation. Shutting a data center is a huge task, and before you even start down the path, it is vital that you can articulate and defend your reasons for doing it. Further, once a data center is shut down, the costs of reopening it can be enormous. From there, data center consolidations are similar to other types of consolidation, except that assessment (especially application, networking, and physical planning) and implementation become much more complex.

Consolidating People Resources and Processes

In any consolidation project, you must not neglect the people and processes you use to manage your environment. Time after time, when we work with clients who have both mainframe and distributed-computing environments, we find that the mainframe side of the house runs smoothly and problem free, while the distributed-computing side of the house is often chaotic, with few developed standards and procedures. The problems that result from this situation demonstrate the importance of resolving these people and process issues. While mainframes consistently run with high availability and high service levels, distributed computing systems often suffer from low service levels and low availability.

Some consulting groups estimate that only 20 percent of data center availability is hardware or technology related; the other 80 percent is estimated to be directly related to people and process issues. The lesson is that successful consolidations must address standards, people, and processes. Without these, availability and service levels may be compromised.

Another benefit of implementing standards and best practices is that you frequently see a 10–20 percent reduction in TCO. You may be able to realize these types of savings by following the recommendations outlined in Chapter 8.

Summary

Consolidation has evolved from being server-centric to including the entire IT environment. This chapter described the different types of consolidation you can perform and provided specific information about the opportunities of each type of consolidation. In addition, this chapter presented general strategies you can use to consolidate servers, applications, storage, shared services, networks, and people resources and processes. Hopefully, it will stimulate you to broaden your horizons, and to look at more opportunities for consolidation.

## CHAPTER 4

Consolidation Methodology

When we first started working on consolidations, we quickly realized that we needed to define a methodology that was simple, complete, and that could be used repeatedly. We needed a methodology that didn't require us to reinvent the wheel each time we started a new project. This sounded like a complex task; however, when we broke consolidation into component parts, it became clear that the individual steps were things that we and our customers do every day.

The methodology discussed in this chapter is generally used for consolidating servers and applications, but the same steps and techniques can be applied to other types of consolidation (for example, storage, network, and shared services consolidations).

This chapter addresses the following topics:

- "Following a Consolidation Methodology" on page 39
- "Completing Project Phases" on page 46

Following a Consolidation Methodology

This section examines the basic methodology that we have followed in our consolidation projects since 1997. While the methodology is based on the simple concepts of assess, architect, implement, and manage, there are several nuances to its application in a consolidation project.

In addition to these four phases, we also include a short, business-oriented assessment at the front end. We call this additional piece a feasibility study because, in many ways, it assesses whether or not a consolidation is feasible.

The following graphic shows the specific areas to address during each of these phases:

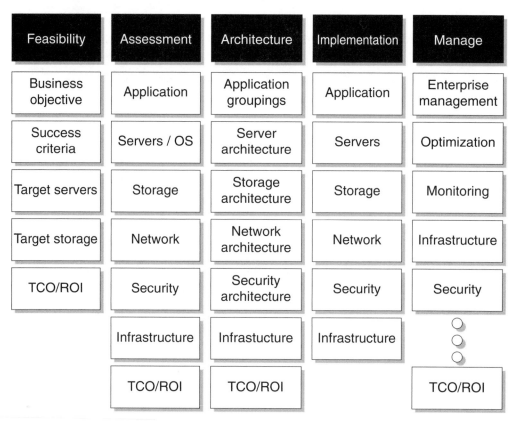

Feasibility	Assessment	Architecture	Implementation	Manage
Business objective	Application	Application groupings	Application	Enterprise management
Success criteria	Servers / OS	Server architecture	Servers	Optimization
Target servers	Storage	Storage architecture	Storage	Monitoring
Target storage	Network	Network architecture	Network	Infrastructure
TCO/ROI	Security	Security architecture	Security	Security
	Infrastructure	Infrastucture	Infrastructure	
	TCO/ROI	TCO/ROI		TCO/ROI

FIGURE 4-1 Detailed Phases of Consolidation

Note — This section of the chapter is devoted to helping you understand the big picture of the overall consolidation process. Specific information about performing the tasks required to complete each of these phases is presented in the chapters dedicated to each of these topics.

Determining the Feasibility of the Project

During this phase, you create a feasibility study that defines the customer's business objectives and the expected results of the project, defines the project scope, and simulates the expected reduction in total cost of ownership (TCO) and the expected return on investment (ROI). The documentation you create during this phase is an essential tool for selling a consolidation project to executive-level decision makers.

Assessing the Current Environment

Assessing the current environment is the most frequently overlooked, yet important phase of an implementation project. During this phase of consolidation, study and document the current environment to provide the basis for the architecture phase of the consolidation project. Because no consolidation environment is a "green-field" data center, this assessment is vital to the success of the overall consolidation. The goal of the assessment phase is to ensure that all of the assumptions made during the business justification phase are proven, and that all of the requirements and dependencies for the architecture are documented. This documentation is the deliverable for the assessment phase of a consolidation project.

To provide complete documentation of the current environment, you must address the following major topics:

- Application requirements
- Platform requirements
- Storage requirements
- Networking requirements
- Security requirements
- Infrastructure and operations requirements

There are two dangers during this phase of the project. The first is that you may perform too cursory an assessment, failing to uncover significant dependencies, which could jeopardize the consolidation viability. This oversight may lead to expensive architectural revisions or even to the failure of the project during the prototyping phase. The other danger is that you may perform too detailed an assessment, wasting time on minutiae that are not relevant to the consolidation. This detailed effort can reduce project momentum and negatively affect the return on investment. Unfortunately, it is difficult for a project manager to judge the depth of the assessment without substantial experience in the environment or other consolidation projects. Information about gauging the level of detail you should apply to the assessment phase is presented in the assessment chapter.

Assess Application Requirements

Application profiling is the most important and difficult part of the assessment phase. Just as the TCO drives the business side of consolidation, application requirements drive the technical side. Because this profiling is so important, we recommend that most assessments begin with this task.

Typical tasks for this part of the assessment include:

- Interviewing application owners and maintainers
- Describing major software components
- Creating a flowchart of network inputs and outputs
- Describing an operational schedule

- Identifying and describing important dependencies
- Creating a road map for the future growth of the application

During this assessment, document all of the various aspects of the application. This documentation is the deliverable for this assessment.

Assess Platform Requirements

Platform assessment has dual purposes. The first is to simply document the hardware and its configuration. The second is to determine its utilization and capacity. While this seems more complicated than application assessment, most of the hard work can be automated.

There are many tools that document systems for you. Of course, in a well-managed information technology (IT) shop, all of this work is already done. Unfortunately, few of us actually work in well-managed IT shops. As such, some kind of system inventory package needs to be deployed. This package can range from simple shell scripts to elaborate framework modules like Tivoli Inventory.

Topics to examine during this assessment include:

- Verifying inventories
- Assessing technical configurations
- Estimating utilization
- Assessing physical environmentals (electrical, footprint, HVAC, etc.)

Security topics are addressed during a separate security assessment.

Assess Storage Requirements

Storage assessment is very similar to platform assessment. In fact, in many consolidation projects, platform and storage assessment might be undertaken as a single task using the same manpower. However, with the burgeoning complexity and sophistication of enterprise storage, we believe this should be a separate task in its own right. This condition is especially true in environments that employ storage area network technology.

Again, the deliverable for this part of the assessment is a report that covers the technical findings, corporate standards, and storage architecture road map for the current environment, as well as a capacity plan.

In addition, you should assess requirements for the following types of storage:

- Online storage of applications and data
- Near-line storage for disaster recovery
- Offline storage for backup

Security topics are addressed during a separate security assessment.

Assess Networking Requirements

When assessing network requirements, gather relevant information about the communications capabilities necessary for server or application consolidations. This information usually involves an assessment of configuration and performance requirements.

Topics to examine during this assessment include:

- For configurations, assess the topology and technologies utilized for the network.
- For performance, assess throughput, bandwidth, and latency. Ideally, you should gather this information for each server or application in the consolidation.

Assess Security Requirements

Consolidated environments can present some complex security problems. Just as platform and storage assessment can be performed as one task, security can be considered part of operations. However, with the ubiquitous Internet connections present in almost every major data center, security cannot be emphasized enough. As such, we recommend that you break security into its own assessment phase. This separation emphasizes security needs and highlights the need for specialized assessment skills.

Security assessment should focus on the following four major areas:

- Security operations
- Security policy and standards
- Security procedures
- Security implementation

The deliverable from this assessment is a written report that addresses the four areas of assessment. This assessment is also a very good candidate for outsourcing.

Assess Infrastructure and Operations Requirements

Infrastructure assessment looks at the intangible parts of the IT environment. This assessment includes the operations, physical environment, and supporting services necessary for the computing environment. Sun PS typically provides a service called Sun Ready Availability Assessment that performs much of this assessment. However, it is important to keep in mind that during this assessment, we are looking forward in the consolidated environment to the future requirements for that environment. We are not looking backward at the needs of the current environment. As such, even the best data centers will be lacking in various areas. For example, if the computing environment consists entirely of department-level servers (like Sun Enterprise 450 servers), the administrators are probably inadequately trained to assess the operational complexities of a Sun Fire 15K server. We feel this assessment is the second most important part of the assessment phase. While these deficiencies should not directly affect the short-term success of the project, they will play a huge role in the long-term success of the consolidated environment. This assessment is often a candidate for outsourcing unless you have significant experience with consolidation.

Document Requirements and Dependencies

Once you complete all of the assessments for an application, create a summary document that contains the high-level requirements and dependencies for the consolidation. Include this information in a recommendation from the assessment team that explains why an application is or is not a good candidate for consolidation. Present this document during a milestone meeting that takes place between the assessment phase and the architecture phase.

Designing an Architecture for a Consolidated Environment

The architecture phase utilizes the requirements and dependencies identified during the assessment phase to design a new consolidated environment. This phase includes the following tasks:

- Creating an initial solution
- Prototyping that concept
- Revising the initial solution
- Documenting the solution

While this is the normal methodology for designing any computing environment, there are some specialized components to this architecture methodology. Most of these components are covered in Chapter 8; however, it is important to understand that this architecture phase may not be as in-depth as it would be if you were creating a "green-field" architecture.

Implementing the Consolidation

Taking the results of the assessment and architecture phases, it is now time to actually execute the consolidation. Careful planning and comprehensive testing are key to the execution of this phase. While this task may appear daunting the first time, it is actually the easiest part of the consolidation.

Most implementation phases can break down into six major tasks. They are:

- **Specify.** For this task, analyze the architecture and identify the hardware and software configurations required to realize it. In many organizations, this is when a "build specification" is created.

- **Build.** With the build specification in hand, install and configure the hardware and software. This task includes physically installing hardware, loading operating systems, and basic testing for applications and functionality.

- **Test.** Testing is the key to the implementation phase. There are two parts to this task:

  - The first part involves testing the built hardware and software to ensure they meet the standards required to begin the migration or consolidation. (This process is probably already a standard within most organizations.)

  - The second task is specific to migrations and consolidations. This task involves testing the migration and consolidation methodology, and requires you to complete multiple runs of migration and functionality testing. You can then script and time the entire migration, or consolidation, to ensure that it can be run within the amount of time you have.

- **Tune.** Tuning for the new platform and operating environment needs to be applied to the application, server, and operation procedures to ensure the new environment works in an optimal mode. This process includes adding resource management tools and techniques to control resource utilization in the new environment.

- **Train.** Administration staff need to be trained on the operation of new equipment, software, and procedures used in the consolidated environment. We recommend that you begin training during the implementation phase, so staff can be useful during the deployment. Oftentimes, training is conducted in concert with the build task of this phase.

- **Deploy.** After building the consolidated environment, training the staff, and testing all migration and consolidation plans, migrate (or consolidate) your environment. This task includes migrating applications and data, as well as testing the new environment.

- **Document.** With the new environment tested and in place, update all old documentation to accurately represent the new environment.

As you can imagine from the preceding description, this phase tends to be heavily dependency-driven. It provides the greatest test of your project management abilities.

Managing the Consolidated Environment

After the consolidation has been implemented and taken into production, there is still plenty of work to do. Managing the consolidated environment often requires dramatically different technologies and procedures than were required by the preconsolidation environment. During this final phase of consolidation, follow the recommendations from the infrastructure assessment performed during the assessment phase, and plug any gaps that have appeared in the new environment.

Completing Project Phases

The key to successfully using this methodology is to complete each phase before you begin the next one. Further, you should always ensure that you not only complete each phase before moving to the next, but that you do so in the order presented in this chapter. To understand the consequences of ignoring these recommendations, consider the following analogy.

Imagine that you are building a new house and you have found the perfect site, and have hired an architect to design your new home. After a short while, you get impatient and take the plans (which are incomplete) to your contractor. The contractor recommends that you wait for the architect to complete the plans, but you want to get started. Responding to your desire to proceed, the contractor pours the foundation and begins framing the house. Then, the architect tells you that he has identified building code issues that necessitate changing the first draft of the plans. Because you didn't allow the architect to complete the planning phase before the contractor began implementing them, and because changes must be made to the original plans, the contractor has to tear out what he has done and must start over. This is an expensive mistake, which is time consuming and frustrating. You would have been better off waiting until the plans were completed.

Consolidation is much the same. If you use a complete methodology and don't stray from it, you'll be successful. If you don't, it's likely that you'll have problems.

Summary

In our experience, a proven consolidation methodology is critical to the success of a consolidation project. In this chapter, we outlined the major phases of the consolidation methodology developed by Sun PS. In the chapters that follow, we discuss the feasibility, assessment, architecture, implementation, and management phases in detail.

## CHAPTER 5

Performing a Consolidation Feasibility Study

The primary goals for a feasibility study include defining the customer's business objectives for consolidation and the expected results of the project, defining the project scope by identifying which servers and storage will be consolidated, and simulating the expected reduction in total cost of ownership (TCO) and the expected return on investment (ROI) for the project.

We designed the feasibility study to be a very short phase, usually lasting one week. In rare instances, when the scope of the project is larger than normal, the feasibility phase may last two or three weeks.

This chapter presents the following topics:

- "Defining Business Objectives" on page 48
- "Defining Success Criteria" on page 49
- "Defining Project Scope" on page 50
- "Identifying the Inventory" on page 50
- "Simulating Total Cost of Ownership Savings" on page 52
- "Establishing a Proof of Concept" on page 63

To illustrate the tasks performed in this phase of the project, we use a sample feasibility study for a fictitious company named Tin Can Networks that provides the initial financial justification for an extensive server consolidation project across multiple data centers. The sample includes a limited feasibility study and a TCO analysis with three scenarios to illustrate various costs and savings. To view the sample feasibility study in its entirety, refer to Appendix A.

Defining Business Objectives

We sometimes find that customers want to do consolidation projects, but that they haven't identified specific reasons for doing so. It is critical to the success of a consolidation that you clearly identify what you hope to achieve from a project. If you can't identify and document the goals of the consolidation, you need to take a step back to reevaluate the reason for the consolidation. Consolidations require a lot of time and money, so it's important that you can clearly articulate your goals. This is especially true when you are trying to sell the project to your C*x*O (chief executive officer [CEO], chief financial officer [CFO], and the like).

The following business objectives are some of the most common objectives we find in projects with which we have been involved:

- Reduce TCO.
- Reduce the amount of floor space used in the data center.
- Increase application availability.
- Reduce the number of servers and instances of the operating system.
- Refresh outdated or obsolete technologies.
- Enable new strategic direction or tactical initiatives.

Whatever your objectives are, make sure that they are crisply defined, well understood, and agreed upon by all project participants.

Sample Business Objectives

For our sample feasibility study, the following business objectives exist:

- Reduce the overall number of servers required to support manufacturing operations to reduce management costs and to reduce the real estate costs associated with housing servers.

- Reduce server maintenance costs.

- Provide a computing environment that reduces downtime and increases server availability to the manufacturing lines.

- Increase the reliability of the computing environment.

- Provide an architecture that increases the transaction volume caused by business growth. This growth is anticipated to be at least 50 percent over the next 12 to 18 months.

Defining Success Criteria

In addition to defining the business objectives for a consolidation project, you must establish criteria for proving that you've met your business objectives. Defining success criteria is not difficult, but it's very important for demonstrating the success of your project to executive sponsors. Success criteria need to be quantitative, not qualitative. You need to be able to numerically demonstrate what you have achieved. Some common metrics include:

- Reducing number of servers in the data center by *nn*%
- Reducing the occupied footprint in the data center by *nn*%
- Increasing availability by *nn*%
- Reducing downtime by *nn*%
- Reducing TCO by *nn*%
- Increasing the ratio of servers per system administrator by *nn*%

Obviously, to establish these criteria, you must be able to access accurate existing performance specifications. While success criteria should reflect the business goals of the project, they must also be obtainable and supportable in the environment where you are implementing them. When establishing these criteria, consider the limitations of your specific environment, as well as the trade offs you must make to implement each item.

For example, you may want to increase availability from 99.99 percent to 99.999 percent, but may also want to reduce costs. Because this improvement to availability requires increased hardware, you will be unable to satisfy both criteria and must negotiate a happy medium.

Most organizations need to consolidate more than one-third of their servers or storage to see significant TCO savings from their projects. We most often see organizations trying to achieve 10:1 to 20:1 consolidations in targeted areas of their inventories, such as file or database servers.

Sample Success Criteria

For our sample, the following quantifiable success criteria were identified:

- Reduce the overall number of servers by 50 percent.
- Reduce floor space usage by 30 percent.
- Reduce server maintenance costs by 20 percent.
- Increase server availability to at least 99.9 percent.
- Increase transaction volume caused by growth of the business. This growth is anticipated to be at least 50 percent over the next 12 to 18 months.

Defining Project Scope

When you define the scope of a server consolidation project, you need to identify all the servers, storage, data centers, and applications that are candidates for consolidation. Hopefully, there is an existing list of all of these candidates that can be used. If not, and if no asset management program is in place, this task includes a tedious and time-consuming physical inventory to gather the necessary information.

When you are ready to start a consolidation, you need to clearly define and limit the scope of your project. For instance, the sample feasibility study used in this chapter focuses on an environment with 500 servers. Once we understand some of the financial implications of consolidating this many servers, we may needed to narrow the scope for the initial project.

For the sample, we carved out a group of about 50 servers based in a single data center that ran some very important applications. By limiting the scope to 50 servers, we are able to commit to our customer's time line of four months to complete the project.

Identifying the Inventory

The project scope is defined as much by what is not included in the project, as what you include in the study. Make sure to explicitly state the assumptions and exclusions to your project. Also state any data sources that are estimated or simulated. For example, if you decide to only re-host servers, make sure to state in the assumptions that this study does not address data center, network, or storage consolidations. Also include the assumptions inherent in the TCO model.

Compiling a Starting Inventory

Compiling an equipment and application inventory can be a very simple or an incredibly difficult task, depending wholly on the size, complexity, and documentation of your current environment. We have seen a full range of methods for inventorying equipment and applications, from clients who have captured this information in database-driven web sites with full querying and reporting capabilities to those who have documented it with simple spreadsheets. The time that is required to gather this data has ranged from 1 week for a customer with about 50 machines to over 5 months for a 600-server, 8-site organization.

If no credible inventory of the environment exists, you have two choices for creating it. You can start from a technical bottom-up approach, or you can start with a business-driven top-down approach. Either approach may be appropriate for your consolidation depending on your project resources and business' organization.

Inventory From the Bottom, Up

The bottom-up approach is appropriate for consolidation projects that are:
- Staffed by information technologies (IT) personnel with few business participants
- For organizations that own all the consolidated assets
- The result of mergers or acquisitions

The bottom-up approach takes an iterative approach to discovering equipment by working from the outside of the data center to the inside. In this approach, we look for a semi-authoritative list of server names and Internet Protocol (IP) addresses, then investigate each one to determine its configuration, applications, and storage. The easiest way to implement this strategy is to dump your organization's Domain Name Service (DNS) tables, and then search out the server entries in it. Other strategies may involve dumping routing tables from your routers, and then conducting "ping sweeps" to find network nodes. Whichever method you choose, this list must be manually verified to ensure that all of the entries are, indeed, possible candidates.

The advantages of a bottom-up approach to creating an inventory is that it reflects the network as it actually is, not how someone thinks it is. The obvious downside to this approach is its long duration and resource-intensive nature.

Inventory From the Top, Down

A top-down approach to creating an application and hardware inventory is based on interviewing the business units to ascertain their current applications. This technique is appropriate for consolidations that are:
- Lead by business users
- Within organizations with decentralized IT management
- Within small or stable IT environments

An interview with business units can be a precursor to the application assessment work, but covers similar ground, albeit at a higher level. This process should produce a list of applications with servers that support its functions. The advantage to this approach is that it takes less time than inventorying from the bottom, up; however, this method may be less accurate without verification.

No matter what approach you take to create your inventory, you need to collect a minimum amount of data. Initially, collect the following information:
- Location of equipment
- Owner information (organization, contact, business unit)

- Server name
- Application information (vendor, version, name)
- Server hardware information (maker, model, central processing unit [CPU] number, type, speed, and network interfaces)
- Operating systems
- Network address
- Storage hardware information (maker, model, capacity, and connection [direct attach, network attached storage, or storage area network])
- Security zone (DMZ, firewall, protected, etc.)
- Clustering

Ideally, this information should be kept in a relational database so that numerous reports can be created from it, but that tends to be overkill for most projects. Usually, you can document the inventory in a small spreadsheet, which still permits you to do some simple analysis on it.

Simulating Total Cost of Ownership Savings

The most important part of the feasibility study is to model your potential TCO savings and ROI. This demonstration of the potential financial impacts of the consolidation is often critical to selling a consolidation to your executive sponsors. The results of this TCO simulation will be similar to those presented in "Understanding Total Cost of Ownership" on page 13.

To perform the TCO simulation, we use Gartner's TCO Analyst software to model the potential TCO and ROI impact of various IT projects. It's not as accurate as an actual TCO measurement, but it's much faster, a lot less expensive, and its accuracy is usually plus or minus 10 percent. For more information about Gartner's TCO measurement software, see "Simulate TCO" on page 17.

Sample TCO Analysis

This initial TCO analysis was performed using Gartner's TCO Manager software and methodology. The analysis is a simulation of expected TCO for a company of Tin Can Networks' size, in Tin Can Networks' industry and in Tin Can Networks' geographic location. The basis for this analysis is Gartner's TCO Index, a database collected from analysis of costs in over 300 data centers in over 200 companies worldwide.

The analysis was performed for the following three scenarios:

- A 33 percent reduction in the number of UNIX servers
- A 50 percent reduction in the number of UNIX servers
- A 67 percent reduction in the number of UNIX servers

In all three cases, the analysis showed a potential substantial reduction of TCO. In each case, the potential ROI was favorable and indicated that the cost of implementing server consolidation was justified by the ROI.

Project Assumptions

For the sample project, we make the following assumptions:

- The TCO analysis performed is a first-cut, rough analysis of the potential savings of server consolidation.
- The server inventory used to determine the current number of servers at Tin Can Networks is from an internal server inventory database. This database is not complete; however, it is the best available source of server population information. A complete analysis, which provides a complete inventory, is performed during the analysis phase.
- Servers include Sun, Hewlett-Packard, and IBM.
- Sun Fire 15K servers are used for the consolidation platforms. Each server and its ancillary hardware is priced at $2,000,000 per server. This cost is only an estimate and does not include discounts or trade-ins.
- The TCO analysis is performed using Gartner's TCO Manager software and methodology.
- No actual costs are collected or used. All results of the simulation are based on the Gartner TCO Index, a database of TCO information derived from over 300 data centers in over 200 companies worldwide. Tin Can Networks' actual costs may differ from this model.
- All indicated cost savings are potential. They are an indication of the types of savings that may be achieved from server consolidation. There is no guarantee that these savings will be achieved.

Business Assumptions

Tin Can Networks background information:

- Annual revenue: $3.5 billion
- Industry: Networking hardware
- Location: Zzyzx, CA (Southwest)
- Number of employees: 20,000

Consolidation Scenarios

Initially, three server consolidation scenarios are analyzed:

- A 33 percent reduction of the current population.
- A 50 percent reduction of the current population.
- A 67 percent reduction of the current population.

The following values are used for initial and subsequent server populations. Servers are categorized based on server cost and depreciation.

TABLE 5-1 Project Server Populations

	Current	Less 33%	Less 50%	Less 67%
Workgroup	285	191	143	94
Departmental	88	59	44	26
Enterprise	5	7	8	9

In the preceding table, the number of servers decreases for workgroup and departmental servers, but increases for enterprise servers because Sun Fire 15K servers are being added to the data center for the consolidation.

The values in the following table are used for the cost of implementing the server consolidation. This table shows estimated implementation costs for each of the three scenarios. The Server Hardware category represents the cost of the Sun Fire 15K servers; the Other Hardware category represents other ancillary costs; the Planning and Implementation category represents consulting costs; and the Additional Costs category is a lump sum for additional contingencies (the things for which you didn't plan).

TABLE 5-2 Consolidation Costs for a 33 Percent Reduction

Less 33%	Initial	Year 1	Year 2
Server Hardware	$2,010,000	$990,000	$0
Other Hardware	$670,000	$333,000	$0
Planning & Implementation	$667,000	$333,000	$0
Additional Costs	$0	$1,000,000	$500,000

Note that the category "Additional Costs" is a general cost category that makes allowance for the inefficiencies of the consolidation process.

The following table represents the same information as is shown in the preceding table, but for a 50 percent reduction.

TABLE 5-3   Consolidation Costs for a 50 Percent Reduction

Less 50%	Initial	Year 1	Year 2
Server Hardware	$3,015,000	$1,485,000	$0
Other Hardware	$1,005,000	$495,000	$0
Planning & Implementation	$938,000	$462,000	$0
Additional Costs	$0	$1,500,000	$750,000

The following table represents the same information as is shown in TABLE 5-2 on page 54, but for a 67 percent reduction.

TABLE 5-4   Consolidation Costs for a 67 Percent Reduction

Less 67%	Initial	Year 1	Year 2
Server Hardware	$4,020,000	$1,980,000	$0
Other Hardware	$1,340,000	$660,000	$0
Planning & Implementation	1,206,000	$594,000	$0
Additional Costs	$0	$2,000,000	$1,000,000

Results of the TCO Analysis

The following table is a summary of scenarios one, two, and three as estimated by the Gartner TCO Manager software, and indicates the estimated TCO savings for each of the three scenarios.

TABLE 5-5   Total Cost of Ownership Analysis for All Scenarios

TCO Analysis Overview	Current	Less 1/3	Less 1/2	Less 2/3
Direct Costs (budgeted)				
Hardware and Software	$9,464,264	$7,119,955	$5,912,957	$4,600,926
Management	$5,887,258	$4,081,673	$3,154,821	$2,150,899
Support	$2,450,322	$1,673,731	$1,275,657	$850,389
Development	$4,405,646	$3,141,017	$2,490,969	$1,781,631

TCO Analysis Overview	Current	Less 1/3	Less 1/2	Less 2/3
Communications	$2,903,170	$2,053,642	$1,617,797	$1,152,403
TOTAL	$25,110,660	$18,070,017	$14,452,200	$10,536,247
Indirect Costs (Unbudgeted)				
End-User IS Costs	$0	$0	$0	$0
Downtime	$1,182,152	$824,833	$641,355	$442,246
TOTAL	$1,182,152	$824,833	$641,355	$442,246
Annual Total Cost of Ownership (TCO)	$26,292,812	$18,894,850	$15,093,555	$10,978,493
Annual TCO per User	$0	$0	$0	$0
Annual TCO per Client	$0	$0	$0	$0
Annual TCO per Asset	$69,558	$73,521	$77,403	$85,105
TCO as a Percentage of Annual Revenue	0.70%	0.50%	0.40%	0.30%
Direct Costs as a Percentage of Annual Revenue	0.70%	0.50%	0.40%	0.30%
Management Staff FTEs	30.9	21.5	20.1	11.5
Users per Network, Systems, and Storage Management FTE	0	0	0	0
FTE Operations and Support Staff	8	5.5	5.2	2.8

The following graphic summarizes the results of this table.

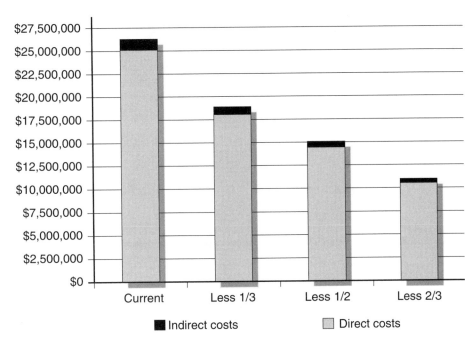

FIGURE 5-1 Comparison of Three Scenarios

Here, you can more clearly see the effect of server consolidation on TCO. This graph indicates that there is a clear advantage of consolidation.

ROI Analysis for Scenario One—33 Percent Reduction

The ROI reflects TCO savings year-over-year. It also indicates whether or not the TCO savings justify the cost of a consolidation and whether the break-even point comes within a reasonable time frame. For information about net present value and internal rate of return, please refer to any commonly used finance or accounting text.

TABLE 5-6   ROI Analysis for Scenario One

ROI Analysis—Typical vs. Target	Initial	Year 1	Year 2	Year 3	Total
Implementation Costs	$3,334,000	$2,666,000	$500,000	$0	$6,500,000
Cumulative Implementation Costs	$3,334,000	$6,000,000	$6,500,000	$6,500,000	
Net Present Value (NPV) of Project Implementation	$6,112,954				
TCO—Typical	n/a	$164,368,805	$164,368,805	$164,368,805	$493,106,415.00
TCO—Target	n/a	$156,970,844	$156,970,844	$156,970,844	$470,912,531
Implementation Rollout	n/a	67%	33%	0%	100%
Adjusted TCO —Target		$159,412,171	$156,970,844	$156,970,844	$473,353,858
Projected Savings	n/a	$4,956,634	$7,397,961	$7,397,961	$19,752,557
Economic Benefits		$0	$0	$0	$0
Savings Plus Benefits	n/a	$4,956,634	$7,397,961	$7,397,961	$19,752,557
Cumulative Savings Plus Benefits	0	$4,956,634	$12,354,596	$19,752,557	
Cash Flow	($3,334,000)	$2,290,634	$6,897,961	$7,397,961	$13,252,557

TABLE 5-6 ROI Analysis for Scenario One *(Continued)*

ROI Analysis—Typical vs. Target	Initial	Year 1	Year 2	Year 3	Total
Cumulative Cash Flow	($3,334,000)	($1,043,366)	$5,854,596	$13,252,557	
Cost of Funds	12%				
Net Present Value (NPV) of Project Cash Flow	$9,475,945				
Internal Rate of Return (IRR)	114%				

The following graphic shows the ROI analysis of scenario one.

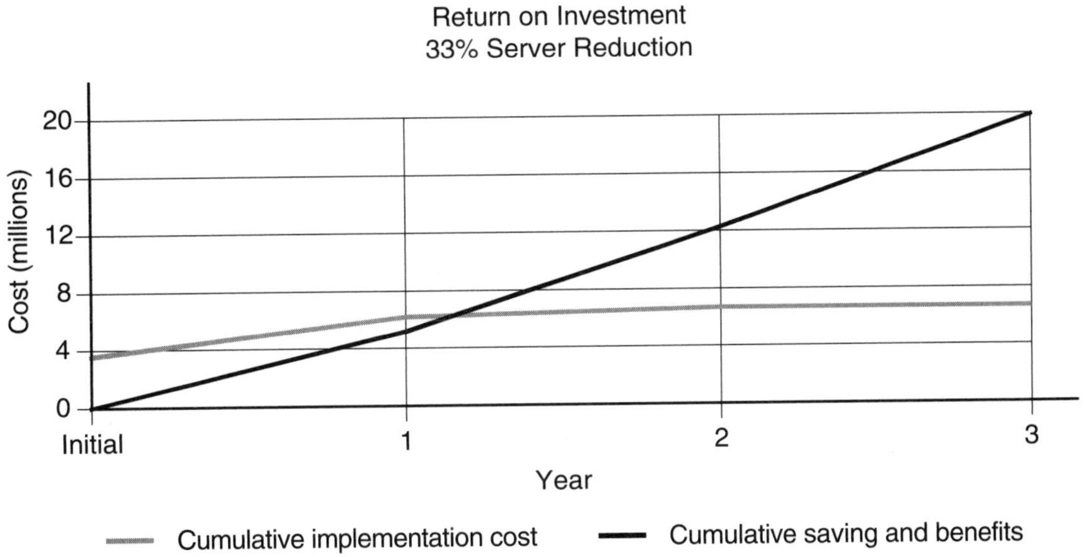

Return on Investment
33% Server Reduction
Cost (millions)
20
16
12
8
4
0
Initial
1
2
3
Year
Cumulative implementation cost
Cumulative saving and benefits

FIGURE 5-2 ROI Analysis—Scenario One

ROI Analysis for Scenario Two—50 Percent Reduction

The following table provides the same information as the preceding table, but for a 50 percent reduction.

TABLE 5-7   ROI Analysis for Scenario Two

ROI Analysis—Typical vs. Target	Initial	Year 1	Year 2	Year 3	Total
Implementation Costs	$4,958,000	$3,942,000	$750,000	$0	$9,650,000
Cumulative Implementation Costs	$4,958,000	$8,900,000	$9,650,000	$9,650,000	
Net Present Value (NPV) of Project Implementation	$9,075,538				
TCO—Typical	n/a	$164,368,805	$164,368,805	$164,368,805	$493,106,415
TCO—Target	n/a	$153,169,548	$153,169,548	$153,169,548	$459,508,645
Implementation Rollout	n/a	67%	33%	0%	100%
Adjusted TCO—Target		$156,865,303	$153,169,548	$153,169,548	$463,204,400
Projected Savings	n/a	$7,503,502	$11,199,257	$11,199,257	$29,902,015
Economic Benefits		$0	$0	$0	$0
Savings Plus Benefits	n/a	$7,503,502	$11,199,257	$11,199,257	$29,902,015
Cumulative Savings Plus Benefits	n/a	$7,503,502	$18,702,759	$29,902,015	
Cash Flow	($4,958,000)	$3,561,502	$10,449,257	$11,199,257	$20,252,015
Cumulative Cash Flow	($4,958,000)	($1,396,498)	$9,052,759	$20,252,015	
Cost of Funds	12%				
Net Present Value (NPV) of Project Cash Flow	$14,523,406				
Internal Rate of Return (IRR)	117%				

The following graphic shows the ROI analysis for scenario two.

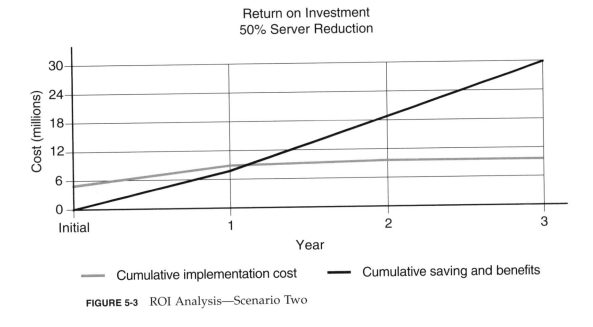

FIGURE 5-3   ROI Analysis—Scenario Two

ROI Analysis for Scenario Three—67 Percent Reduction

The following table provides the same information as TABLE 5-6, but for a 67 percent reduction.

TABLE 5-8   ROI Analysis for Scenario Three

ROI Analysis—Typical vs. Target	Initial	Year 1	Year 2	Year 3	Total
Implementation Costs	$6,566,000	$5,234,000	$1,000,000	$0	$12,800,000
Cumulative Implementation Costs	$6,566,000	$11,800,000	$12,800,000	$12,800,000	
Net Present Value (NPV) of Project Implementation	$12,036,408				
TCO—Typical	n/a	$164,368,805	$164,368,805	$164,368,805	$493,106,415
TCO—Target	n/a	$149,054,487	$149,054,487	$149,054,487	$447,163,460
Implementation Rollout	n/a	60%	40%	0%	100%

TABLE 5-8   ROI Analysis for Scenario Three *(Continued)*

ROI Analysis—Typical vs. Target	Initial	Year 1	Year 2	Year 3	Total
Adjusted TCO—Target		$155,180,214	$149,054,487	$149,054,487	$453,289,187
Projected Savings	n/a	$9,188,591	$15,314,318	$15,314,318	$39,817,228
Economic Benefits		$0	$0	$0	$0
Savings Plus Benefits	n/a	$9,188,591	$15,314,318	$15,314,318	$39,817,228
Cumulative Savings Plus Benefits	n/a	$9,188,591	$24,502,909	$39,817,228	
Cash Flow	($6,566,000)	$3,954,591	$14,314,318	$15,314,318	$27,017,228
Cumulative Cash Flow	($6,566,000)	($2,611,409)	$11,702,909	$27,017,228	
Cost of Funds	12%				
Net Present Value (NPV) of Project Cash Flow	$19,276,601				
Internal Rate of Return (IRR)	114%				

The following graphic shows the ROI analysis of scenario three.

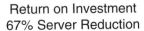

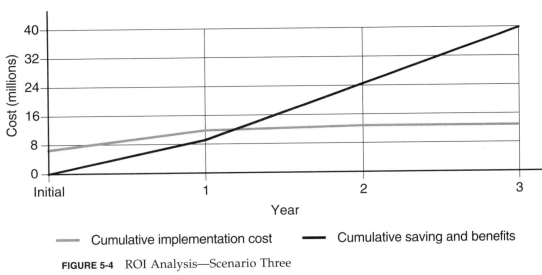

Return on Investment
67% Server Reduction

FIGURE 5-4 ROI Analysis—Scenario Three

Conclusions From the Sample Project

Based on these preliminary analyses of the various scenarios, both TCO and ROI strongly support this server consolidation project. Increasingly aggressive levels of consolidation should produce increased savings to Tin Can Networks.

Establishing a Proof of Concept

In addition to the tasks involved in developing a feasibility study, you should also consider the importance of being successful with your first consolidation project. Successfully establishing a "proof of concept" for consolidation is essential to gaining support for future projects. One of the ways you can do this is to limit the scope of the first project you undertake.

For example, you may have several hundred or several thousand servers that you want to consolidate, but you shouldn't try to consolidate them all at once. We have found that limiting your first consolidation to 40–60 servers results in a project that can be completed within a reasonable period of time, with a high degree of success.

The importance of success in the first consolidation project cannot be overestimated. If the first one works, you will gain support for additional consolidations. If it fails, you probably won't get a second chance.

Consolidations of 40–60 servers can last anywhere from four months to one year. Four months is very fast; one year is probably too long. Six months is an average time frame for a project of this size.

Identifying a Group of Servers to Consolidate

When identifying which servers to consolidate, ask for a list of servers in the data center, including common server characteristics such as the number of CPUs, CPU speed, memory, and average and peak utilization rates. Very often, we find that customers cannot give us this information; they just don't have it. If you cannot access this information, determine whether you want to proceed to the assessment phase or whether you want to select a different set of servers about which you have this information.

In any case, when you choose the first group of about 50 servers to consolidate, the best strategy is to pick the "lowest hanging fruit." Pick the servers and applications that seem to be the best candidates for consolidation, leaving the more difficult ones for a later project. Examine the patterns presented in Chapter 3, as well as any unique patterns you have identified in your own environment to identify which consolidation candidates can be plugged into the patterns.

Identifying the Initial Storage to Consolidate

Remember that you get a storage consolidation with a server consolidation. If you are going to reuse your existing storage, you simply need to ensure that there is enough I/O capacity, and move the storage to the new consolidation server. If you are going to change your storage architecture, you need to determine which type of storage architecture you will use for the consolidation. Most commonly, you will consolidate to a storage area network (SAN). You may also consolidate to a heterogeneous connect architecture. Or, you may use a combination of the two. Here again, you want to pick the easiest consolidation candidates. Once you have demonstrated success and have some experience under your belt, you can tackle the more difficult candidates.

Now that we better understand the potential for consolidating this large group of servers, we need to repeat the process for our initial group of about 50 servers and the attached storage that we mentioned earlier in the chapter.

A TCO simulation of the proposed initial project showed the following expected TCO and ROI results.

TABLE 5-9   TCO Analysis for Sample Project

TCO Analysis Overview	Typical	Target	Target-Typical	% Difference
Direct Costs (Budgeted)				
Hardware and Software	$2,882,864	$926,703	($1,956,161)	-68%
Operations (Formerly Management)	$870,168	$235,817	($634,351)	-73%
Administration (Formerly Support)	$175,638	$45,153	($130,485)	-74%
Total Direct Costs	$3,928,671	$1,207,673	($2,720,997)	-69%
Indirect Costs (Unbudgeted)				
End-User Operations (Formerly End-User IS)	$0	$0	$0	–
Downtime	$264,982	$50,650	($214,332)	-81%
Total Indirect Costs	$264,982	$50,650	($214,332)	-81%
Annual Total Cost of Ownership (TCO)	$4,193,652	$1,258,323	($2,935,330)	-70%
Total TCO as a Percentage of Annual Revenue	8.40%	2.50%	-5.90%	-70.00%
Total Direct Costs as a Percentage of Annual Revenue	7.90%	2.40%	-5.40%	-69.30%

The following table shows the ROI analysis for the sample project.

TABLE 5-10   ROI Analysis for Sample Project

ROI Analysis (Target vs. Typical)	Initial	Year 1	Year 2	Year 3	Total
Implementation Costs	$4,650,000	$0	$0	$0	$4,650,000
Cumulative Implementation Costs	$4,650,000	$4,650,000	$4,650,000	$4,650,000	$4,650,000
Net Present Value (NPV) of Project Implementation	$4,650,000				
TCO—Typical	n/a	$4,193,652	$4,193,652	$4,193,652	$12,580,956
TCO—Target	n/a	$1,258,323	$1,258,323	$1,258,323	$3,774,968

TABLE 5-10   ROI Analysis for Sample Project *(Continued)*

ROI Analysis (Target vs. Typical)	Initial	Year 1	Year 2	Year 3	Total
Implementation Rollout	n/a	100%	0%	0%	100%
Adjusted TCO—Target		$1,258,323	$1,258,323.00	$1,258,323	$3,774,968
Projected Savings	$0	$2,935,330	$2,935,330	$2,935,330	$8,805,989
Economic Benefits		$0	$0	$0	$0
Savings Plus Benefits	$0	$2,935,330	$2,935,330	$2,935,330	$8,805,989
Cumulative Savings Plus Benefits	$0	$2,935,330	$5,870,659	$8,805,989	
Cash Flow	($4,650,000)	$2,935,330	$2,935,330	$2,935,330	$4,155,989
Cumulative Cash Flow	($4,650,000)	($1,714,670)	$1,220,659	$4,155,989	
Cost of Funds	12%				
Net Present Value (NPV) of Project Cash Flow	$2,400,166				
Internal Rate of Return (IRR)	40%				

Even this initial project, with a very limited scope, projected very favorable TCO reduction and ROI.

Summary

This chapter explained how to create a feasibility study that defines the business objectives and expected results of a consolidation project, defines the project scope by identifying what will be consolidated, and documents the expected reduction in TCO and the expected ROI. Throughout this chapter, a sample feasibility study was used to illustrate these points.

## CHAPTER 6

Planning a Consolidation Project

Once the hard work of justifying and selling the business case for consolidation has been completed, the job of delivering on this promise awaits. What seemed so simple during the feasibility phase, now looks daunting and near impossible. It is likely that you will ask yourself, "How will we ever consolidate these servers given the time, resource, and availability constraints?"

This is where project planning comes into focus. Consolidation projects can be complex undertakings that span several years. Without proper planning and management, it will be easy to lose course; however, with proper planning and management, consolidation can be a relatively painless and rewarding exercise. The key to success lies in two important requirements: a solid methodology and strong project management.

This chapter details the tasks involved in taking the next step in consolidation—planning a consolidation project. While the preceding chapters focused on creating a business case and justifying it to company management, this chapter begins the journey of making it reality. It takes you through a detailed methodology for consolidation, focusing on important project activities and milestones. To illustrate our points, we create a sample project plan. Additionally, this chapter presents methods for identifying and assembling the technical skills necessary to execute a project plan.

This chapter addresses the following topics:

Creating a Project Plan

This section details methods for constructing a realistic project plan for a consolidation effort. This section details the specific tasks you must complete for each phase of the methodology and explains the benefits of creating milestones to track your progress. Special attention is given to critical "decision" milestones and executive-reporting activities. These tasks include:

- Defining consolidation objectives
- Clarifying project scope
- Assessing consolidation candidates
- Estimating and documenting time lines
- Identifying high-level project phases
- Setting major milestones
- Developing a project plan
- Estimating realistic project durations
- Reporting project status

In this section, we illustrate our points using a sample project plan for a typical consolidation. While we understand that no consolidation project is typical, our sample covers most legacy consolidations. In the example, we consolidate approximately 50 older workgroup-level UNIX servers running 15 applications to a pair of Sun Enterprise 10000 servers running the Solaris Operating Environment (OE). Also, we centralize 10 Windows NT file servers into one of the domains with the PC Netlink product, and we consolidate the applications, as well as the major application's storage, on two EMC Symetrics arrays.

Defining Consolidation Objectives

As discussed during the feasibility sections of this book, it is vitally important that you clearly define and document the objectives of the consolidation project. Defined too broadly, the project will never finish. Defined too narrowly, it will not realize true cost savings and efficiencies for the organization.

While you may need to refine objectives during project planning, most of the objectives should be clearly defined during the business feasibility phase. Most of the work, here, should be adding supporting objectives to the plan.

The "sweet spot" in defining business objectives is to combine the two parts of the server consolidation puzzle, technical and financial, into one cohesive statement. You should then follow this objective with supporting objectives that define a general approach.

These objectives lead to an obvious set of critical success factors for the project. Again, you can divide these into financial and technical categories. For each of these success factors, identify an instrumentation mechanism for evaluating the factor. For example, if the critical success factors are:

- Financial
  - Lower support costs
  - Decrease contract costs
  - Decrease floor space utilization

- Technical
  - Increase system processing capacity
  - Increase application availability

Then the instrumentation of the consolidation should include:
- Budgets
- Data center floor measurements
- System performance and capacity data
- Application availability statistics

Setting objectives that cannot be measured will doom a project to failure.

Clarifying Project Scope

While the preceding paragraphs detailed what to include in a project plan, it is equally important to communicate what is not part of a project. As with all ambitious projects, "scope creep" can be a dangerous adversary. To avoid creating a project that has too broad of a scope, clearly define the items that are out of the scope of the project. For example, if you are consolidating a three-tier web infrastructure that interfaces with a back-office mainframe, you might want to specifically exclude the mainframe. Likewise, if you are consolidating the direct attached storage, you might want to specifically exclude the network attached storage (NAS) that you recently installed.

Assessing Consolidation Candidates

With the objectives and the scope defined, it is time to set a general approach to the project to decide which candidates to begin with, and which candidates to consolidate together. The three major rules, here, are as follows:

- **Follow a phased approach.** Make sure there is a phased approach to the project, grouping sets of applications that should be consolidated at the same time. These might be applications that will reside on the same instance of the operating system or that have dependencies on one another. Don't think that you are going to consolidate the entire data center in one "big bang." Approach it slowly at first, concentrating on one small application system. Make sure that everyone participates in this first consolidation. As you gain more experience, you can run multiple consolidations in parallel. We refer to this as a "waves" approach.

- **Avoid impacting users.** Start with consolidations that impact the user the least. Do not start your consolidation project with any server or application that has the term "critical" applied to it. Find something small, simple, and redundant. Perfect choices include things like print or file services. While these might not be simple or "noncritical" services in your company, for the most part, they are redundant.

- **Consolidate self-contained waves.** Everything that is needed to complete an application wave needs to be part of the wave's project plan, or needs to be completed before the wave starts. This condition specifically refers to storage consolidations. Many people break storage out into its own wave and expect it to have little effect on application consolidations. This belief cannot be further from the truth.

Estimating and Documenting Time Lines

Once you have come up with a general approach, put it down on paper. Diagram the waves using educated guesses for durations. Take a look at the overlaps, and imagine some of the dependencies that you might be creating.

For our sample consolidation project, we create seven application waves, one for each domain on the two Sun Enterprise 10000 servers. Before the waves begin, we define a feasibility phase. We estimate the duration of that phase to be 30 elapsed days, then prioritize each wave from least to most important. (Storage consolidation is handled during each of the application waves.) For this example, we estimate each wave to last eight weeks. This time frame allows three weeks for assessment, three weeks for architecture, and two weeks for implementation. While this is an aggressive schedule, it is doable in our fairly simple example. The Gantt chart that reflects this information should appear similar to the following example:

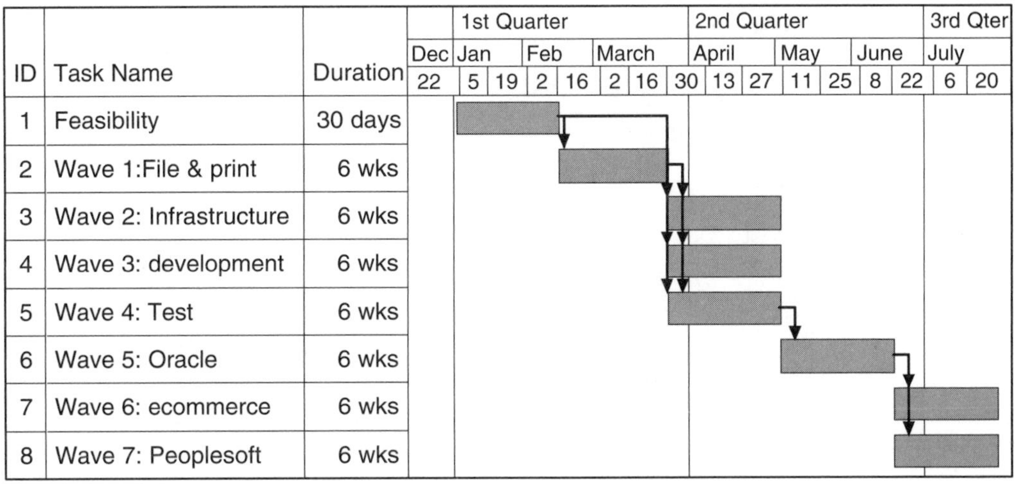
ID
Task Name
Duration
1st Quarter
2nd Quarter
3rd Qter
Dec
Jan
Feb
March
April
May
June
July
22
5
19
2
16
2
16
30
13
27
11
25
8
22
6
20
1
Feasibility
30 days
2
Wave 1:File & print
6 wks
3
Wave 2: Infrastructure
6 wks
4
Wave 3: development
6 wks
5
Wave 4: Test
6 wks
6
Wave 5: Oracle
6 wks
7
Wave 6: ecommerce
6 wks
8
Wave 7: Peoplesoft
6 wks

FIGURE 6-1 Initial Time Line Estimates

In this example, we use the file and print services as a pilot wave. Then, we make sure to get the infrastructure, development, and test consolidations out of the way. With these in place, the Oracle consolidation domain can be installed. Finally, we schedule the most complex waves, which contain the e-commerce and PeopleSoft applications. In this approach, each wave's dependencies are addressed in a preceding wave. Most of the dependencies are technical in nature. In our example, for instance, it might be important to have the Oracle and storage waves in place before attempting the PeopleSoft consolidation.

Once you feel comfortable with your high-level approach, it's time to start to set milestones, and to define each of the assessment phases.

Identifying High-Level Project Phases

After you establish the objective and approach for the project, you can start populating the project plan with the high-level phases of the project and with the major milestones of the project. As explained in the preceding chapters, it is very important to follow a definitive sequence in consolidations, and to avoid starting one step before completing the prior one. As such, the project phases introduced in Chapter 4 are perfect starting points for high-level activities.

Within each of our waves, the activities become:

1. Assessment

2. Architecture

3. Implementation

4. Management

5. Closure

For now, we stick with our original estimation of six weeks per wave, leaving the management and closure tasks as simple milestones. Later in the development of the project plan, we will decide whether the management and closure tasks should be addressed within each wave or all at once. In the meantime, adding this information to our project plan expands it to appear as follows:

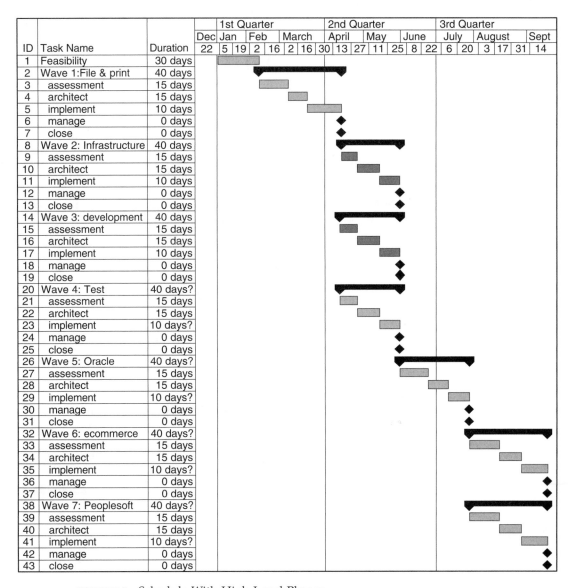

ID	Task Name	Duration
1	Feasibility	30 days
2	Wave 1:File & print	40 days
3	assessment	15 days
4	architect	15 days
5	implement	10 days
6	manage	0 days
7	close	0 days
8	Wave 2: Infrastructure	40 days
9	assessment	15 days
10	architect	15 days
11	implement	10 days
12	manage	0 days
13	close	0 days
14	Wave 3: development	40 days
15	assessment	15 days
16	architect	15 days
17	implement	10 days
18	manage	0 days
19	close	0 days
20	Wave 4: Test	40 days?
21	assessment	15 days
22	architect	15 days
23	implement	10 days?
24	manage	0 days
25	close	0 days
26	Wave 5: Oracle	40 days?
27	assessment	15 days
28	architect	15 days
29	implement	10 days?
30	manage	0 days
31	close	0 days
32	Wave 6: ecommerce	40 days?
33	assessment	15 days
34	architect	15 days
35	implement	10 days?
36	manage	0 days
37	close	0 days
38	Wave 7: Peoplesoft	40 days?
39	assessment	15 days
40	architect	15 days
41	implement	10 days?
42	manage	0 days
43	close	0 days

FIGURE 6-2 Schedule With High-Level Phases

Setting Major Milestones

Once the high-level actives are in place, look at the business-driven milestones for the project. These milestones are markers for significant business interests. Common examples of business-driven milestones include:

- Retiring old hardware
- Deploying new applications or services
- Budgetary cycles

While some of these are phase-change milestones that relate to the waves (for example, completion of wave 1), some of the business-driven milestones apply to the entire project (for example, the retirement of old hardware). For example, if the objective of a consolidation project is to migrate all applications off of leased hardware to return it without renewing the lease for another year, you would add two milestones to the project plan: one for the lease renewal data, and another for the date when the machines can be returned.

In addition, put another set of milestones in place for executive reviews. These milestones usually follow the phase-change milestones, but could pop up at other times. For example, when the architecture is nearing completion, executives might want a central architecture committee or standards board to review it. Examples might include auditing or purchasing reviews within certain phases. These milestones will vary depending on your organization in politics and policies.

For our sample project plan, we add the business-driven milestones of our lease renewal and machine return. During the assessment and architecture phases, we include milestones for executive and financial reviews (identified in lines 4 and 6 in the following schedule). Finally, we add milestones within the implementation phase for end-user sign-off of the consolidated environments (line 8 in the following example). The following example shows each phase of the first wave (file and print) schedule, including milestones:

ID	Task Name	Duration	1st Quarter					2nd Qtr
			Jan	February		March		April
			19	2	16	2	16	30
2	Wave 1:File & print	40 days						
3	assessment	15 days						
4	assess review	0 days						
5	architect	15 days						
6	arch review	0 days						
7	implement	10 days						
8	enduser signoff	0 days						
9	manage	0 days						
10	close	0 days						

FIGURE 6-3 Phases of First Project Wave

Developing a Project Plan

With the high-level structure of the project set, drill down to the details of these tasks. Luckily, these tasks are largely the same for each wave; however, durations of the tasks differ depending on the complexity of the consolidation. At this stage of the project plan, we still assume that all of the waves are similar in complexity.

Define the Assessment Phase

We start by drilling down into the first high-level task, assessment. The following categories are commonly addressed in the assessment phase:

- Application
- Platform
- Storage
- Security
- Infrastructure
- Summary

In addition, we break out capacity assessment (line 7 in the following graphic) from the platform and storage assessments. We isolate this task because it takes special skills and tools, and may require separate resources. Based on experience, we estimate durations for the tasks and add them to the sample project plan.

ID	Task Name	Duration	1st Quarter				2nd Qtr
			February		March		April
			2	16	3/2	16	30
2	Wave 1:File & print	40 days					
3	assessment	15 days					
4	application	4 days					
5	platform	4 days					
6	storage	2 days					
7	capacity	5 days					
8	security	3 days					
9	infrastructure	5 days					
10	summary	1 day					
11	assess review	0 days					
12	architect	15 days					
13	arch review	0 days					
14	implement	10 days					
15	enduser signoff	0 days					
16	manage	0 days					
17	close	0 days					

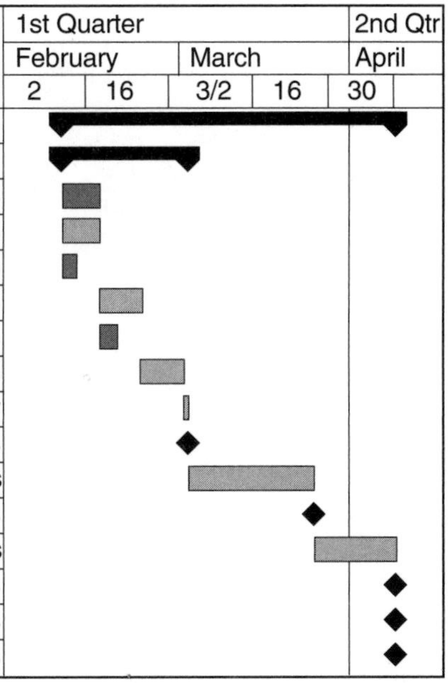

FIGURE 6-4 Detailed Categories and Time Estimates for Assessment Phase

Define the Architecture Phase

With the assessment tasks in place, move on to the architecture phase. In this phase, we add the following tasks:

- Reviewing the requirements that were gathered during the assessment phase
- Developing an initial design
- Building a prototype
- Revising the design
- Documenting the design

These tasks may be different at your company, depending on your company's standards for architecture and design. Some organizations have very rigid standards for this, while others have almost none at all. In addition, tasks vary greatly depending on the complexity of the consolidation. The three-week duration in this example is overkill for a simple file and print server architecture, but might be a gross underestimation for the PeopleSoft environment.

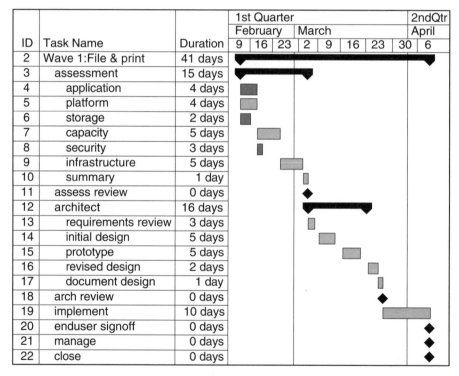

ID	Task Name	Duration
2	Wave 1:File & print	41 days
3	assessment	15 days
4	application	4 days
5	platform	4 days
6	storage	2 days
7	capacity	5 days
8	security	3 days
9	infrastructure	5 days
10	summary	1 day
11	assess review	0 days
12	architect	16 days
13	requirements review	3 days
14	initial design	5 days
15	prototype	5 days
16	revised design	2 days
17	document design	1 day
18	arch review	0 days
19	implement	10 days
20	enduser signoff	0 days
21	manage	0 days
22	close	0 days

FIGURE 6-5 Detailed Categories and Time Estimates for Architecture Phase

Define the Implementation Phase

Once the architecture is completed and approved, the real work of the consolidation begins. This effort consists of the typical environment build-out, including the following tasks:

- Specifying and procuring hardware, software, and network components
- Building a consolidated environment
- Production testing the consolidated environment
- Deploying the consolidated environment

In addition to these tasks, it is especially important to allot time for documenting the consolidated environments, and for training staff on the new environment. These items are often overlooked in simple, nonconsolidated environments.

The following graphic reflects each of these implementation tasks:

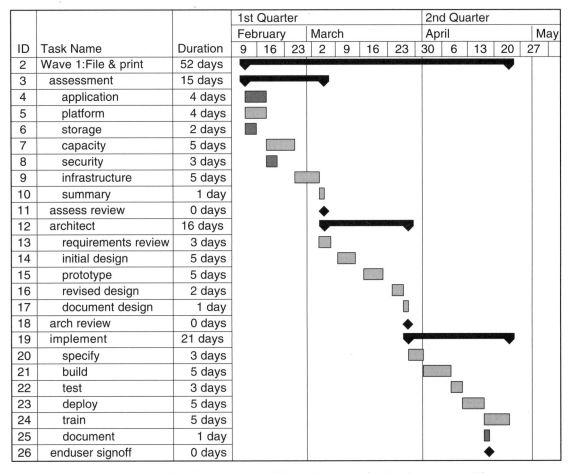

FIGURE 6-6 Detailed Categories and Time Estimates for Implementation Phase

The wave ends at the completion of its implementation phase. All the other phases are structured just as they are in this phase, but with varying levels of effort, depending on the complexity of the consolidation.

Define the Management Phase

The management phase examines the entire environment, independent of the wave, application, or technology. During this phase of the project, put an infrastructure in place to help manage the newly consolidated environment. These items might be processes that were found to be insufficient during the infrastructure assessment, or software to help monitor the new systems. Whatever your infrastructure entails, it needs to be addressed during this phase of the project.

In the sample project, we are unsure what we need to address at this point; however, we can safely say that we need to include new monitoring tools for the Sun Enterprise 10000 server to look for performance and fault problems. We add these tasks to the project plan for now, leaving room for other items that will become apparent during the assessment and implementation phases. Our project plan now appears as follows:

ID	Task Name	Duration	May 25	June 1	8	15	22	July 29	6	13	20	August 27	3	10	17	24	September 31	7	14	21	Oct. 28	5
59	Management	15 days																				
60	Implement monitoring tools	15 days															▨▨▨			▨		
61	Revise change procedures	15 days															▨▨▨			▨		

FIGURE 6-7 Initial Categories and Time Estimates for Management Phase

Note that we scheduled the management phase to begin as late as possible in our project plan. We will keep it here for the initial planning, but will reassess the schedule after completing the first wave.

Complete the Project Cycle

With the management phase of the project complete, the formal consolidation methodology is finished. However, in a consolidation project, it is especially important to bring proper closure to the project. Because cost avoidance is the basis for many consolidations, you need to analyze whether savings will come to pass. For some consolidations, simply completing the project shows the savings (perhaps in instances where leases are involved). However, in most consolidations, you need to feed the project information to the accounting department so that true savings can be tracked.

For the closure of most projects, you should create a summary report that compares planned durations with actual durations, and summarizes the financial costs and savings of the project. In addition, your summary report should include a "lessons learned" (both good and bad) section as a basis for best practices in the next consolidation project.

Estimating Realistic Durations

Estimating realistic duration times for each task in a consolidation project is essential to producing a schedule you can meet, and to securing the confidence of those requesting the consolidation. While it may seem difficult to estimate realistic duration times for tasks that you haven't performed before, you can simplify the process by recognizing the similarities between tasks performed during a consolidation project, and tasks that are common to core competencies. For example, look at the implementation phase of the project. During this phase, you specify, build, test, and deploy a system. While it is a consolidated system, the steps are quite similar to the normal process used to roll out a new environment. The only unknown part of the equation is the level of difficulty being introduced by layering more complexity into the environment.

With this in mind, it is a little easier to estimate durations for the tasks involved in a consolidation project. Knowing that it usually takes three days to implement a server in a data center, you can surmise that it might take a full week to implement a moderately complex consolidated server. The tried-and-true method of doubling time estimates can be surprisingly accurate in this case.

Reporting Project Status

Reporting is especially crucial for consolidation projects. Because they are highly visible within an organization, it is important that you effectively communicate the status of any consolidation project. To be an effective communication tool, reporting needs to be:

- **Pertinent.** Project reports should be relevant to their readers. For example, you shouldn't forward system administrators' bug tracking notes to nontechnical readers who have no basis for evaluating the importance of the bug, and who may elevate the seriousness of the problem in their minds. Instead, consider summarizing the issue and report the status of the problem's resolution; do not report the solution, but report the progress that has been made towards solving it.

- **Consistent.** Project reports should be distributed at set intervals in a standardized format. Allow readers to see the progression of a task or phase being planned, executed, and completed.

To ensure that information is pertinent to the audience reviewing it, we recommend you create two types of reports: executive and participant.

- **Executive report.** A high-level report geared towards the completion of the project and the progress being made to satisfy business goals. This report mostly consists of milestones and task statuses, but also includes budgetary numbers for project expenses.

- **Participant report.** A lower-level report that is technically oriented. This report includes a discussion of deliverables, problems encountered during the project, and schedule changes. Oftentimes, project teams review this report during weekly meetings.

Identifying Resource Profiles

After detailing tasks and durations in a project plan, you should identify the resource profiles required to complete the tasks. Resource profiles are sets of skills that are required to accomplish groups of tasks within a project plan. For example, assessing the current platform and building the new platform are two separate tasks, which require similar skills. To accomplish either task, you must have a resource who understands the hardware and operating system technologies used in a particular environment. Once you identify all of the resource profiles for a particular project, you can assign resources with these profiles to individual tasks, and begin the project.

Identifying a Project Manager

The first resource profile is the project manager. No matter how small a consolidation is, a project manager is vital to the success of the project. There are simply too many scheduling, logistical, and administrative issues to deal with to have a technical resource "moonlight" as the project manager. Someone needs to be dedicated, if only part-time, to this role.

The manager must be experienced in large-scale, complex projects. Most consolidation projects have terribly complex dependencies and even more difficult logistics. Corporate politics and executive visibility further compound these problems. Inexperienced or unskilled project managers may be more easily defeated by these challenges than those who have significant experience in this area.

Identifying Resources to Assess Requirements and Architect Solutions

The next role is the subject matter expert (SME) architect. There will probably be several of these people within the project—one or more per subject. In our example project, we need an expert for the server, an expert for applications, and an expert for the storage. We might also need an expert to address security issues, depending on the company. Each of these resources have separate profiles, even if we were lucky enough to find one person who might be able to satisfy more than one of them. Architects need to have a great deal of experience with the subject matter, but must also understand higher-level issues like scalability, which are inherent in design. People who fit this role carry out the assessment and architecture phase, with some consulting during the implementation phase.

Identifying Resources to Implement and Administer a Project

Consolidation projects also need SMEs who are implementers and administrators. These people are similar to the SME architects, but are charged with implementing the consolidated architecture and managing it. As such, there is a need for relevant low-level technical skills and experience. These people tend to be the current environment's system administrators.

The areas that require SMEs vary depending on the nature of the project. In our sample consolidation project, we should look for SMEs in storage area networks (SANs), databases, enterprise servers, data center operations, and security.

Organizing Your Project

While our sample project is very simple, some consolidations can be grand in scope. In fact, many companies are looking at consolidating data centers around a region. It is not uncommon for organizations to want to cut the number of servers, so that they can reduce the number of physical sites that operate. Organizing a consolidation of this magnitude requires a bit more management overhead than our example.

In situations like this, we suggest you create a program office. The idea behind creating a program office is to impose a meta layer over the entire consolidation effort. As each consolidation is its own project, complete with managers, staffs, and plans, someone needs to coordinate the dependencies between the projects, liaison with appropriate outside parties, and keep executives sponsors up-to-date. In addition, a technical authority needs to ensure that each project follows assessment and architecture standards. However, conflict resolution between the separate project groups in the overall consolidation is, by far, the most important duty for the program office.

An example of this would be a company looking to centralize their data center operations into one major site, while keeping another site as a backup. They currently operate data centers in most of the major Pacific Rim cities, but have chosen to centralize their operation in Beijing, China (close to their manufacturing plants) and Singapore (their corporate headquarters). While each data center would have its own project plan and project crew, a program office should be formed to coordinate their activities and report to the sponsors. In addition, a program office could serve as a communications hub for each group's activities with business users and other consolidation teams.

Ideally, a program office is composed of program managers, administrators, and architects. A program manager is in charge of the overall consolidation project. This manager coordinates project plans, reports progress, and serves as a liaison with other parts of the business (especially business users). A technical architect should be available to assist the program manager. This architect can set the technical vision for the project, as well as establish architectural standards for environments. This person ensures that similar design choices are made across a project. Program managers work directly with local consolidation project teams, in a consultative manner to ensure that the vision and standards are being applied.

In addition to a program manager and technical architect, a program office should have a project administrator. This administrator is responsible for the communication, organization, and documentation of the project that aren't formally assigned elsewhere. Tasks for this position include gathering status reports, reporting on project expenses, and handling logistics.

With the program office in place, create the supporting structures. Structures may vary depending on the particular organization and project needs, but most projects' organization charts are similar to the chart shown in the following graphic.

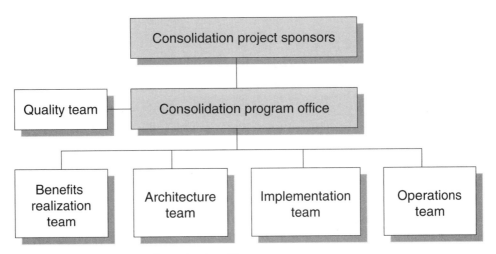

FIGURE 6-8 Project Team Organization Chart

The supporting teams for the project usually include the following roles and responsibilities:

- **Quality team.** This team monitors the overall project process and outputs, and reports results to the program office. This monitoring may range from simple project reviews, to full-scale audits. The program office includes the quality team's results in its communications with the project sponsors and implementers.

- **Benefits realization team.** This team ensures that the project meets its goals. This team is involved in many phases of the project, from feasibility, to implementation (procurement), and to management (staffing). Most of this group is comprised of IT managers and accountants who must approve the technical decisions being made by the architecture team.

- **Architecture team.** In charge of the overall design and specifications of the consolidated environment, this team carries out most of the architecture phase of the project.

- **Implementation team.** This team builds, deploys, and migrates the consolidated environments. This team is usually a rotating group of subject matter experts with the skills required for the particular consolidation.

- **Operations team.** This team is in charge of scheduled migrations and downtime in the current environment.

In consolidations with many waves, there might be several architecture and implementation teams, due to scheduling and technical requirements.

Summary

This chapter explained the importance of properly planning for a consolidation project. Through the use of a sample project, this chapter presented the tasks involved in creating a project plan. In addition, this chapter provided information about identifying and securing essential project resources.

## CHAPTER 7

Assessing Technical Feasibility

This chapter details the technical assessment phase of a consolidation project. This phase proves the preliminary work of the feasibility and project planning phases, and gathers information used to establish key requirements during the architecture phase. Applications, servers, storage, and networks are analyzed in detail during this phase. In essence, this is the "due diligence" for a consolidation project.

While most of this phase concentrates on gathering data, the analysis of the data is the real deliverable from this phase. As hard as it might be, make sure that the process of gathering data doesn't obscure your analysis of it. We have seen many project schedules slip because too little time was scheduled for analyzing data in medium to large consolidations.

For the most part, the methodology and techniques described in this chapter apply to all consolidations. However, don't hesitate to deviate from these tasks if you are consolidating networks or data centers. For example, analyzing floor space, air conditioning, and electrical requirements for a data center consolidation may be a substantially different undertaking than physically consolidating several older, large servers into smaller "blade" servers.

The following tasks provide a minimum practice for consolidation assessment:

Preparing for the Assessment

Before beginning the assessment phase, lay some groundwork to ensure that you assess the correct servers, arrays, applications, and environments. If you have gone through a formal feasibility phase, you should have covered most of this at that time. At the very least, you should have an inventory of all applications, servers, and storage in the environment, with the potential servers to be consolidated identified. If you do not have this information, it needs to be prepared before you continue. Unfortunately, this may be a project in itself for many organizations. For more information, refer to "Identifying the Inventory" on page 50.

Profiling Applications

Application profiling is by far the most important part of the overall assessment process. As consolidations are always either business or application driven, this should be fairly obvious; however, many times we find that this isn't the case.

The objective of application profiling is to understand exactly what the application is being used for, how it operates, and who uses it. In organizations where this activity is routinely documented as part of the software development cycle, the application profiling phase is very simple. However, in most organizations, applications have grown "organically," with few documents stating their goals, operations, or users. In these environments, you must gather this data yourself.

The primary tasks involved in application profiling include:
- Documenting data flow
- Identifying dependencies
- Assessing application portability
- Documenting the profile

Documenting Data Flow

You can begin to create an application profile by understanding and documenting how data flows through an application. By this, we mean you should understand how data moves from process to process, or from machine to machine, to accomplish specific tasks. You don't need to document every feature of the application, but you do need to understand the most important ones. These tasks should include three major categories: user, administrative, and batch.

By understanding how data flows through an application, you can map the interaction between users and processes. This step also provides you with a glimpse of how possible consolidations can be attempted. While you can use special tools to determine application flow, we find that it is often just as helpful to sit down with someone who is knowledgeable about the application.

The result of this small task should be a diagram that contains both representations of processes, as well as data flows or actions. Oftentimes, developers or system administrators already have this kind of documentation. If not, you might also be able find it with the software vendor, if the application has been purchased. Regardless of how you obtain this documentation, it is vitally important that you document and fully understand the application flow.

To illustrate this point, we use a simple e-commerce application as an example. Suppose that you run a small retail web site. As part of the small web site, you have several front-end web server applications, a set of application servers, and a database server back end. Because you already have a system inventory and a simple network diagram, you can infer a few things about the application. These include:

- Each server runs some kind of appropriate application.
- The front-end web servers accept traffic from users.
- The application servers talk to the front-end web servers and the back-end database.
- The back-end database only talks to the application server.

By adding the processes (on the web and application servers) and arrows that represent communications to our diagram, the basic application structure is now mapped as follows.

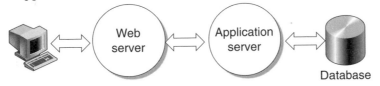

FIGURE 7-1   Basic Application Mapping

Armed with this diagram of assumptions, you need more information from people who are familiar with the application. Oftentimes, these are the people who administer the application (system administrators) or the developers of the application (developers). Whoever they are, you need them to help delve deeper into the application's workings. In our example, we trudge off to meet with the system administrator to better understand the application's setup. We ask them the following questions to verify our diagram:

- Does our diagram depict all of the appropriate servers?
- Does our diagram identify all of the major processes?
- Are the communications correct?

While asking these types of questions, make sure to prompt your interviewee to cover all aspects of the application's use, including batch and administrative. Many people forget to include important administrative details (like backups and such), which can result in an incomplete set of requirements for the architecture phase.

Once you have verified the diagram map, delve deeper into each process and communication line that you have drawn. For each process, you might ask the following questions:

- What, specifically, is this application?
- What is its major function?
- Is it purchased or developed?
- What versions of the application are installed?

This should provide information about the specific implementation that the architecture is running. You also need to delve into communication lines. Some questions may include:

- What protocol is this communication?
- What port (assuming Transmission Control Protocol/Internet Protocol [TCP/IP]) does this communication run over?
- What is the content of this communication?

Applying this information to our example, we found a number of interesting things in our conversations with the system administrator:

- The five front-end web servers primarily run Sun Open Net Architecture (Sun ONE) web servers (version 3.6) and accept incoming TCP communications on ports 80 (Hypertext Transfer Protocol [HTTP]) and 143 (secure HTTP).

- The web servers communicate with the application servers through a custom NSAPI application (written in-house) over nonprivileged port 25001.

- The application servers are running Sun ONE application servers version 6.1.

- The back-end databases are running one instance each of Oracle 8.1.5 and communicate with the application server by using SQL*net on the normal ports.

By adding this information to our diagram, we have a fairly good overview of what our application is composed of and how it operates. Our sample application diagram now appears as follows:

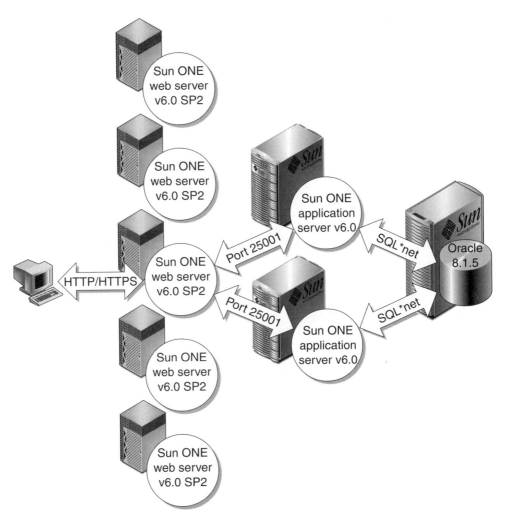

FIGURE 7-2 Sample Application Process Diagram

At this point, you need to decide how far you want to profile the application. The level of detail depends on the complexity of the consolidation you're assessing. For purely physical consolidations, you might not have to delve into much more detail than we already have; however, for more complex consolidations (such as most logical consolidations), you'd want to look deeper to identify more specific details. In our sample, we want to be able to consolidate the application server and the database back end. Because this is a fairly complex consolidation, we definitely need to gather more information. The key question to ask yourself when deciding whether you have enough information about the application is, "Do I have enough information to architect this design on a new consolidated server?"

Identifying Dependencies

Once you understand how data flows through an application, look into the components and configuration of the application. While you should document these lower-level details, you want to look specifically for dependencies within the application's implementation. These dependencies could be as simple as a hard-coded host name, or as complex as interprocess communications. Most commonly, it will be a limitation on the supported operating environment version.

To examine an application for this level of detail, examine inventories of application configurations, and interview administrators and developers. When examining inventories, harvest the configuration files of your application, and ensure that you understand all of the processes involved with it. Of course, this process assumes that you know what these configuration files are and where they are stored.

Use Process Accounting Tools

One way to make sure that you include all processes in this assessment is to use a process accounting tool, which is built into the operating system. Process accounting tools record all processes, as well as system utilization on a server. This tool comes at a reasonably small price, using less than 5 percent central processing unit (CPU) utilization, but provides a wealth of detail in the form of daily, weekly, and monthly reports.

▼ To Enable Process Accounting on Your Server:

1. **Check that the Solaris Operating Environment (Solaris OE) accounting packages are installed.**

```
# pkginfo | grep SUNWacc
system      SUNWaccr      System Accounting, (Root)
system      SUNWaccu      System Accounting, (Usr)
#
```

2. **Enable the accounting startup files (as** root**).**

```
# ln -s /etc/init.d/acct /etc/rc2.d/S22acct
# ln -s /etc/init.d/acct /etc/rc0.d/K22acct
```

3. Add the following entries to the adm **user's** crontab.

```
0 * * * * /usr/lib/acct/ckpacct
30 2 * * * /usr/lib/acct/runacct 2> /var/adm/acct/nite/fd2log
30 7 1 * * /usr/lib/acct/monacct
```

Solaris OE process accounting provides regular reports listing all the processes executed during the proceeding period. In addition, the lastcomm(1) command can show you this information on demand.

Interview Developers and Architects

When you interview application developers or architects, make sure that you cover topics such as the following:

- Release levels
- Service level agreements
- Operations
- Users
- Code
- Software quality
- Testing
- Development
- Road map

The objective of these interviews is threefold. You want to:

- Gain valuable requirements information for the architecture phase.
- Nail down configuration details for the implementation phase.
- Highlight any possible dependency problems.

While the first two objectives are fairly self-explanatory, the third can be a bit tricky. Dependency problems are details that tie application architecture to the underlying hardware architecture, for example, a dependency on a piece of peripheral hardware. In our sample, dependencies might include a Secure Sockets Layer (SSL) accelerator card for web servers, or a special analogue communication line that the application server uses to verify credit card details.

Software versions are another example of a dependency. Perhaps the application server only runs on the Solaris 7 OE, but has not yet been certified under the Solaris 8 OE. You must understand all of these details very well before you enter the architecture phase. In fact, sometimes, these dependencies disqualify a seemingly perfect application from a consolidation project.

Assessing Application Portability

Now, we face another decision point. Again, we are going to evaluate whether or not we need to go deeper in our assessment of the application. However, this time the decision hinges on whether we need to port this application to another operating environment. If we are going to port the application from one operating environment to another (even to a virtual environment like Java™), we are going to need to look at code and scripting level topics. Otherwise, it is time to document our findings and move on with the assessment phase.

If the product was purchased, not developed in-house, some research on the product is in order. The first place to start would be with the vendor who can tell you whether or not a version of the application exists for the desired (new) platform. Assuming that the application runs on the platform, there should be a fairly easy path to migrate your data to it. However, if there is not a version for the new platform, you need to revisit the decision to migrate or choose a new solution.

While most of the actual details of migrating applications from one environment to another are out of scope of this book (Sun has plenty of good books about porting applications to the Solaris OE or to the Java environment), there is an assessment that needs to be done first. The first step to this assessment is to understand the current developing environment and tools. This assessment was probably done during the last task (application interview), but it would be wise to go back over the results in detail now—especially if unfamiliar products are being used. The second step would be to inspect the current source code base. It should be fully versioned, somewhat documented, and most importantly, fully buildable. If the code can't be built on the current platform, there is little logic in porting the code to a new platform. The final part of porting assessment would be to judge its complexity to port. For this task, you need helpful tools or expert advice.

Documenting the Profile

The final step of the application profiling process is to document the results. This documentation should include all the information gathered during the assessment (starting with our diagram), the people interviewed, and a short summary of the high-level requirements. In addition, any dependencies should be highlighted.

Assessing Platforms

Once the application profiles have been completed, look at the infrastructure supporting them in more detail. This information is the second leg of the table, so to say. Luckily, there are far more tools to automate this assessment task than the last.

The three major goals of this part of the assessment are to:
- Verify inventory
- Assess and understand technical configurations
- Estimate utilization

While these goals are somewhat far reaching, we will limit the scope of this assessment to the machines that support the applications we assessed. This assessment still may be a daunting task, depending on the how well the inventory and application profiles were completed.

Verifying Inventories

The easiest way to begin assessing platforms is to verify the inventories and application profile reports that we completed for each machine. Hopefully, every machine described in the application profile report appears on the inventory. If not, it is time to put on your detective hat and start laying hands on machines to see which is correct. Assuming that the machines and inventory match, you should start digging deeper into the technical configurations of the machines.

Assessing Technical Configurations

When assessing the technical configuration of a system to be consolidated, group the information into four categories:
- Server hardware
- Operating environment
- Storage and backup
- Networking

The server hardware information is fairly ordinary. The type of information you should gather includes:
- Machine make and model
- Processors (quantity, type, speed, and cache sizes)
- Random access memory (RAM)
- Peripheral cards
- Boot information (OpenBoot™ software settings on Sun hardware)

Most of this information is important to do an accurate sizing, but the peripheral cards can be a major roadblock to migrating to another vendor or model. Other than the peripheral cards and boot information, you should already have it on the inventory.

The operating system information is the most detailed, but the easiest to automate. At this point, focus on gathering information to replicate the environment on a new server. This information should consist of:

- Operating environment name and version
- Kernel patch level and important patches
- Naming options like Domain Name Service (DNS) servers, Naming Information Service (NIS) servers, and the name switch file (/etc/nsswitch.conf on the Solaris OE)
- System administration tools and versions.

This should represent all of the information that is needed to reinstall and reconfigure the operating environment on a new server.

Automate the Assessment Process

Ideally, digging into the configurations should be an automated process. With a configuration management system in place, this is definitely the case. Solutions like Pergrine Infratools and Tivoli Inventory can relieve project staff from much of the highly manual inventorying tasks, while increasing accuracy. As a bonus, these tools can also provide ongoing reports in case the consolidation has significant time delays between phases.

Without a commercial solution in place, you'll need to find other ways to automate this assessment. An easy way to automate technical assessment information gathering in a Solaris OE is to implement the Explorer package. Explorer is a configuration-information gathering script developed by Sun's Support Services division to populate the support help desk line database. However, it can be used just as well by any organization to gather information about their servers.

Installing the Explorer package is straightforward and simple. Download the package from the SunSolve℠ web site (http://sunsolve.sun.com/) and execute the pkgadd command. This task automatically adds a crontab entry to run the script weekly. For more customized information gathering, modify the crontab entry to run only certain Explorer modules.

Explorer automatically outputs a gzipped tarball of file contents and command outputs. By centralizing these Explorer tarballs in a common directory, simple perl or shell scripts can extract details for spreadsheets or reports.

Estimating Utilization

As the final part of the assessment, estimate the current resource utilization of the platform. There are several ways to do this, with both built-in system commands and third-party performance software suites. While the built-in commands are free and easy to use, for most consolidation projects you should consider using performance software suites for their capacity planning capabilities.

System Activity Reporter

The simplest way to collect system utilization information is with the built-in system activity reporter (SAR). SAR has been staple of the Solaris OE since the days of SunOS software, but it still gets the job done for basic tracking of CPU and disk utilization data. It creates daily reports on CPU, memory, disk, and other resources by sampling utilization at regular (usually 20-minute) intervals. The report can then be examined to estimate the peak utilization of important resources within the system. While SAR allows you to estimate the utilization of important resources, it does not allow you to create models of the system for future capacity planning exercises. Any modeling or capacity planning will need to be done by hand, usually with the help of spreadsheets.

Performance Software Suites

Performance software suites provide a more comprehensive approach to utilization data collection. In addition to collecting data, these suites include programs to graphically view the data (either on the web or through a graphical user interface), to monitor systems, and to model changes to the system. This modeling software is the key differentiator between performance software suites and other monitoring software. Performance modeling software constructs system models based on gathered performance data to predict how the resource will react under differing loads. As you can imagine, this information is incredibly useful for server or storage consolidation efforts.

There are several performance software suites available for UNIX platforms. Prominent among these packages are TeamQuest Corporation's TeamQuest software and BMC's Perform and Predict software. Both provide excellent support of the Solaris OE. Through the course of this book, we use TeamQuest software to illustrate examples of capacity planning. The TeamQuest software suite includes numerous tools for simplifying capacity planning. Performance data can be monitored or recorded with extensive reporting features. The TeamQuest TQ Model program can take recorded utilization data, organized into workloads, to create system performance models.

To use TeamQuest, install the agent software on each monitored machine. This installation is a simple process, similar to using the Solaris OE pkgadd command. Once the software is installed, you need to define system workloads. Workloads categorize your performance data so you can isolate just the data for the applications or processes that you will consolidate. This is a straightforward process, assuming that you have process accounting reports handy. Using the TeamQuest Admin program, create workload definitions through regular expressions. For example, you might want to create a workload for all the web server processes. To define this workload, create a workload called "webserver" that is defined by the expression:

```
uid == 60001 OR gid == 60001
```

This expression categorizes anything running with user ID 60001 (the nobody user) or the group ID 60001 (the nobody group) as part of the "webserver" workload. Reports in the TeamQuest View tool allow you to see utilization data categorized by workload. Create workloads for all discrete applications that exist. These workloads will be the foundation of capacity planning exercises in the architecture phase of the project.

To estimate resource utilization, analyze the data or graphs output from the tool to find the peak of the resource utilization data. This process requires at least one, if not several weeks, of data collection by the tool. It is easiest to do this step using some kind of graphical tool, like TeamQuest's View. The following graphic shows data collected by TeamQuest over one week.

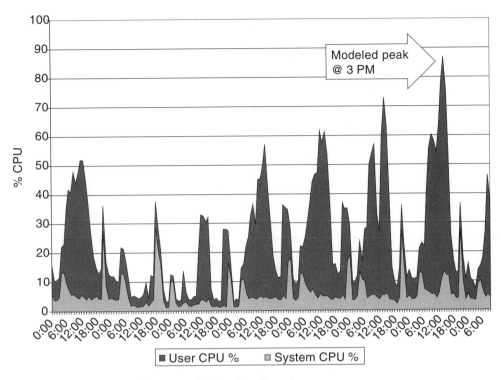

FIGURE 7-3 TeamQuest Resource Utilization Report

This peak period (towards the far right side of the graph) shows that the system processing power is approximately 88 percent utilized around 3:00 p.m. Using this data point, you can create a system model within the TeamQuest TQ Model tool during the capacity planning section of the project. To gather that information for later use in the TeamQuest Model tool, use the TQGETM program to create a model input file. The TQGETM program is a simple text based tool that extracts system configuration and resource utilization data from the TeamQuest monitoring database. For this example, we specify the peak period identified earlier:

```
# ./tqgetm
TQGETM 8.2 SP-2   (US/Pacific) Wed Jul 17 12:34:55 2002
Copyright (c) 2001-2002 TeamQuest Corporation.  All Rights
Reserved.

Enter configuration file name </opt/teamquest/etc/tqgetm.cfg> :
Configuration file '/opt/teamquest/etc/tqgetm.cfg' will be
created.

Enter output file name </opt/teamquest/bin/ezrec.abr> :
Output file '/opt/teamquest/bin/ezrec.abr' will be created.

Enter start time (hhmmss <000000>) :150000
Enter length of time (hhmmss <010000>) :

Enter start date (mmddyyyy <07172002>) :05202002
Enter number of days <1> :1

Aggregation Set "8-hour" has been selected.
You requested a time period with an elapsed time of 01:00:00
(hh:mm:ss).
   With Aggregation Set "8-hour", data is available for 06:15:57
(hh:mm:ss).

CPU Utilization        : 41.14%
Disk I/Os per second : 13.60
Do you want to use this date and time period? (Yes or No) :YES

Selection : <05/20/2002 15:00-00:00>
Enter model title :hyrax

Workload :
  List of available workload sets for Workload.
     1: Example          2: webserver
  Enter index or name <1 : Example> :2

(continued on next page)
```

```
(continued from preceding page)
Data selection values.
Title       : hyrax
System      : hyrax
Agg Set     : 8-hour
Database    : production
WLS         : webserver
Start time  : 15:00
End time    : 00:00
Start date  : 05/20/2002   (mmddyyyy)
End date    : 05/20/2002   (mmddyyyy)
Interval    : 06:15:57

Generating report to output file '/opt/teamquest/bin/ezrec.abr'

End TQGETM
#
```

Store the model input file until the architecture phase of your consolidation project.

Assessing Storage

When we first started consolidations, storage was almost an afterthought, addressed during the platform assessment tasks; however, over the past five years, storage has grown in technologies, complexity, size, and importance. In fact, storage consolidation tends to be the most popular consolidation these days. With this growth in complexity and importance, it is important to treat storage assessment with a little more care and respect than we have given it in the past.

The key point of this part of the assessment is to separate storage (hardware and technologies) from data (actual stored information). This process is similar to the comments in the preceding section about servers. We need to understand both the possible capacity of the hardware, as well as what is actually being utilized. To facilitate this understanding, gather configuration information, as well as utilization information like performance and storage capacity.

There are three types of storage to assess during this phase of the project. These include:

- **Online storage.** This is where servers store their applications and data. Whether these are directly attached, storage area network (SAN)-attached, or network-attached, you need to account for them the same way.

- **Disaster recovery (or business continuity planning) storage.** This storage is the off-site storage that is utilized in case of an emergency. It can be considered as near-line storage.

- **Offline or backup storage.** Most commonly, this storage takes the form of Digital Linear Tape (DLT) libraries attached to a particular server or to a centralized backup server.

Of course, while most environments have all three of these types of storage, some might not have backup or disaster recovery storage, depending on the environment's configuration.

Another key to storage consolidation is to recognize that all storage is not accessed equally and often requires varying degrees of reliability, availability, and serviceability, as well as performance. Simply adding up the amount of current storage and throwing it into a large pool, or large storage array subsystems, could lead to an implementation nightmare. Each application should be inventoried or profiled for its requirements, and only then, should the decisions about storage consolidation be made.

The process for assessing storage is very much like the process for assessing platforms. You need to discover the storage in the environment (by now, this is an easier task because the application profile and platform assessment might already be done), gather information, and analyze the information for subsequent reports. Before the recent introduction of several tools specifically for managing storage, this was a manual process. We will demonstrate the Sun StorEdge Resource Management Suite software as an example of the tools available for potential consolidations.

Analyzing Online Data

We will look at online storage first, as it is the easiest about which to gather information. We basically look to answer the following questions about online storage:

- Online configuration
  - What houses the data?
  - How do servers access the data (for example, with direct-attached, network-attached storage [NAS], or SAN)?
  - Which servers access the data?
  - What solutions are in place for data resiliency (for example, a redundant area of independent disks [RAID])?
  - What is the volume layout?
  - Which file systems, if any, are used for the data?
- Online data utilization
  - What types of data are being stored?
  - Who owns the data?
  - How large is the data?

- How old or recently used is the data?
- How often is the data revised?
- Are any application performance issues associated with storage?
- Are there measured performance statistics for the data (IOPS [I/Os per second], kilobytes per second transferred, and reads or writes per second)?

Analyzing Near-Line Data

For near-line storage, we usually ask a similar, but slightly different set of questions. These should include:

- Near-line configuration
  - How are data backed up in this environment?
  - Are any archival storage practices in place?
  - Is an hierarchical storage management solution in place?
  - Do you have a disaster recovery plan?
  - Is there an implementation of the disaster recovery plan?
  - What houses the data?
  - How do servers access the data (for example, with direct attached, NAS, or SAN)?
  - Which servers access the data?
  - What solutions are in place for data resiliency (for example, RAID)?
  - What is the volume layout?
  - Which file systems, if any, are used for this data?

- Near-line utilization
  - How does the near-line storage differ from the online storage in data types, capacities, and use?
  - Any other questions that compare near-line storage to online storage, as they should be very similar.

Analyzing Offline Data

Offline data storage is a very different type of storage to assess. While we will need to look into the same major topics, the questions will be very different.

- Offline configuration
  - What houses the data?
  - How do servers back up data?
  - How do servers restore data?
  - What software is used to back up and restore data?
  - What is the offline data volume?
  - How long is offline data retained?
  - How long is offline data retained inside the on-site housing?

- Online data utilization
  - What types of data are being stored?
  - Who owns the data?
  - How large is the data?
  - Are there legal requirements to keep data?
  - How long do you have to back up data?

Automating Storage Assessment

Sun StorEdge Resource Manager software enables organizations to proactively discover, monitor, and manage their storage and data through a centralized tool. It provides charts and graphs of current, historical, and future trends about data. While it can entirely automate the online aspects of this assessment, it only provides indirect information on the near-line and offline storage.

The software operates with a client-server model like most monitoring products. A local agent (installed on each server) monitors the data and storage devices utilized by that server. A centralized server then aggregates and reports this information. A variety of reports can be produced through the product, including reports about:

- Space
  - Total available and used space
  - Space available and used by the file system
  - Space trending graphs by the file system
- Files
  - Distribution by size
  - Distribution by access date

In addition, Sun StorEdge Resource Manager software can gather inventory information about the servers and storage devices themselves. While this tool cannot automate the complete storage assessment, it significantly increases the speed and accuracy of the assessment.

Assessing Networking Requirements

Network assessment is designed to gather relevant information about the communications capabilities necessary for server or application consolidations; however, it is also necessary for most storage consolidations given the rise of NAS and new IP-over-SAN technologies. Whatever the consolidation type, it usually makes sense to take the time to perform at least a casual assessment of the network.

Network assessment follows two standard areas: configuration and performance.

- **Configuration.** For configuration, mostly look for the topology and technologies utilized for the network. For most local area networks (LANs), this means determining whether servers use Fiber Distributed Data Interface (FDDI), 100BASE-T Ethernet, or possibly asynchronous transfer mode (ATM). For wide area networks (WANs), this means asking the networking department about T1s, E1s, Integrated Services Digital Network (ISDN), and frame relay. The important pieces to gather here are the topology and the link speeds.

- **Performance.** For performance, there are three main points to gather: throughput, bandwidth, and latency. Ideally, you should gather this information for each server or application in the consolidation.

The key point in network assessment is understanding how much to assess. In this assessment, you need to look for both scope (the size or number of elements being assessed) and depth (the amount of information and calculation needed to understand performance). As an example, if you are consolidating several servers within a single data center, you probably don't need to assess much more than the LAN between servers and their clients. Likewise, you probably have little need to characterize the client's change in response time because the server may only be moving over a subnet, or so. However, if you are centralizing and consolidating servers from around the region or globe, you'll have a considerable task ahead of you. You will need to catalog the speed of every link between the client and new server position, and will probably want to calculate, simulate, or pilot the latency of the new client connections.

To understand the importance of network assessment, consider the following incident from an actual server consolidation. In this project, network assessment was targeted for elimination from the project for the sake of time. The organization had a solid network topology—all data center servers were connected to ATM-capable switches on a single virtual local area network (VLAN). These Ethernet switches, in turn, were connected to switches on the company's ATM core. The network people had been told that the data center's 43 machines were to going to be replaced by two machines, making the network even simpler; however, the Sun Enterprise 10000 server domain feature complicated the picture. Between that news and a new network backup strategy, it was clear the network was going to need to be looked at more closely. Our network assessment followed the Open Systems Interconnection (OSI) networking model, examining everything from physical wiring through naming and addressing, to application protocols. Of special concern was performance. Basic traffic models were derived from information gathered from switches by network management system (NMS). In the end, a new backup network utilizing Gigabit Ethernet was installed to off-load traffic from the client networks.

Assessing Security

The security assessment phase is designed to understand the application's or server's security requirements and to understand how they are being implemented. It is neither designed to assess an application's or server's resistance to penetration, nor is it designed to assess the quality of its implementation. The idea behind this assessment is to be able to document the information needed to either architect a new solution or re-implement the server on new hardware.

Just as we have presented the assessment goals as two parts, most organizations divide this information between two sources. The first source is usually the information security policy for the application or company that was drafted by the organization's security department. It will be a high-level document that defines the types of information and protections that are needed to be applied to certain data or actions. The more detailed part of this assessment, the security implementation, will usually be in the application or server architecture document, and will be drafted by the security officer or architect working on the application itself. This part consists of the methods, procedures, and tools used to comply with the data security policy.

Assessing Infrastructure and Operations

The infrastructure and operations review is a very important, but often overlooked, part of the assessment phase. In building any consolidated environment with high levels of performance and reliability, people, processes, and tools are extremely important. In fact, in recent articles focusing on reliable data centers, independent consulting groups estimate that of these three factors, technology represented only 20 percent of the final result. The other components, people and process, represent the remaining 80 percent.

This infrastructure review is a high-level examination of an organization's data center infrastructure, with an emphasis on people, process, and tools. The objective of the assessment is to complete an analysis of the data center's strengths, to identify areas for improvement and potential risks, and to develop specific recommendations to be completed before consolidating an environment. There are several ways to approach this assessment. One popular method is to interview key people and review relevant documents.

The assessment process benchmarks the data center against the following key data center disciplines:
- Data management
- Software management

- Network management
- Security
- Disaster recovery
- Performance management
- Change management
- Asset management

These disciplines effectively segment the functions of a data center into eight components providing a compartmentalized perspective of the overall IT architecture. This compartmentalization is neatly aligned to an optimal data center organizational structure, thereby permitting the assessments and recommendations to fall into logical boundaries of responsibility. Each functional segment identifies the specific criteria that must be properly addressed to ensure that the process under examination enables fast and flexible strategies, while maintaining a reliable architecture.

Of course, this method is not the only way to assess your data center. Several other data center management models exist, most notably the Information Technology Infrastructures Library (ITIL) service delivery methodology. As long as you apply a consistent methodology and focus your assessment on strengths and weaknesses for the coming consolidation, it shouldn't matter what model you use.

Revaluating Total Cost of Ownership

As you have worked your way through this technical assessment of your environment, you have undoubtedly found that some of the consolidation scenarios outlined during the feasibility phase are not possible. This may be due to political, technical, or logistical reasons. Due to the unfortunate law of nature, you need to revisit the financial analysis, and update it with newer, more educated assumptions about consolidation feasibility.

This revised financial analysis may prove that the proposed consolidation does not meet the success criteria. This outcome either provokes a reevaluation of the proposed consolidations (perhaps leading to a more aggressive consolidation), or it leads to the end of the project. This financial analysis should be evaluated in isolation. Your project plan should include a milestone at the end of the assessment phase milestone to decide whether it is appropriate to continue with the project. When you reach this milestone, consider all of the information gathered up to this point.

Assessing Risk

Any project has its share of risk associated with it. Consolidations are no different. Moving applications, data, or data centers to new locations or hosts provides the opportunity for any number of problems to break out. As the final part of your assessment phase, identify and quantify possible risks.

The first step of this work would be to identify the possible risks in your consolidation. These risks might include:

- Financial
- Security
- Availability
- Data integrity

The next step is to identify possible sources of risk in your consolidation. These risks might include:

- Project length
- Project complexity
- Staff skills
- Experience
- Business unit support
- Executive support
- Incomplete data
- Project scope
- Project management

After finishing these steps, weigh the risks against the possible rewards you identified during the business justification, and make a qualitative analysis of the potential to consolidate. There are several ways to do this, one of which is to use a third-party tool from one of the analyst groups. The Standish Group has a tool called the VirtualADVISOR Risk Assessment Model, which can help you quantify the likelihood that a project will succeed or fail. This tool works on a survey basis, assigning points to various factors to rank the overall risk of a project. Another way to evaluate risk is to audit the proposed consolidation. Audits identify risk, quantify it, and suggest methods to mitigate risk.

Whichever method your organization uses to identify and evaluate risk, make sure to include it in the overall assessment of your consolidation project.

Summary

This chapter explained how to perform the tasks you must complete before you can design a consolidated architecture. These tasks included compiling a starting inventory, profiling applications, assessing requirements (of platforms, storage, networks, security, and infrastructure and operations), and assessing risk.

## CHAPTER 8

Designing a Consolidated Architecture

In the architecture phase of the consolidation effort, information from the feasibility and assessment phases of the project is used to design the consolidated solution. This phase of the project is usually a five-step process, including the following tasks:

- "Creating an Architecture" on page 109
- "Prototyping the Initial Solution" on page 128
- "Revising the Solution" on page 130
- "Documenting the Solution" on page 130

Each of these steps builds upon previous work to progress the design along to the implementation phase. Reliable and accurate data are essential to producing a reliable and accurate architecture.

Creating an Architecture

Architecture takes high-level requirements and defines the structure of a system by identifying the important components and their relationships to solve the problem at hand. It focuses on communications and interactions, and on overall system organization. Good architecture identifies the key problems facing the system, and solves them before it is implemented.

Solutions architecture is not the implementation or specification of the system. It does not call for specific hardware or software, much less versions or patch levels. It is concerned with where data are stored, instead of what kind of array is used for storage. It is ensuring that there is sufficient processing power to sustain 1000 users, not defining the low-level detail such as deciding to use four 900 megahertz central processing units (CPUs). These low-level details are defined when you create the specifications for building the consolidation during the implementation phase of the project. The tasks involved in this phase include:

- Extracting requirements from data
- Addressing common consolidation design issues
- Addressing specific consolidation architectures
- Sizing the consolidated architecture

There are several ways to conceptualize system architecture. At Sun, we have embraced a methodology called the SunTone[SM] Architecture Methodology. It conceptualizes system architecture as a cube, where the differing faces of the cube represent system tiers, layers of the stack, and systemic qualities of the solution.

While we have talked at a fair length about the tiers of the system (presentation, business, integration, and resources), we have not spent much time talking about the layers or the systemic qualities (or "ilities," as they are called in the following graphic).

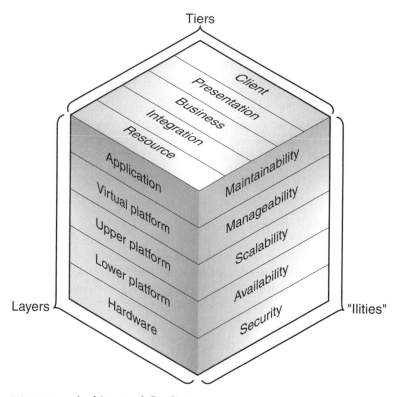

FIGURE 8-1 Architectural Qualities

The preceding graphic represents the following information:

- The layers of the SunTone Architecture model represent the hardware and software that support the different tiers. This is the "stack" to which many architectural white papers refer.

- The hardware layer consists of the different physical elements within the architecture. These might be servers, arrays, switches, or routers.

- The lower platform represents the operating environments and utilities that host applications.

- The upper platform is comprised of applications such as front-end servers, application servers, and middleware products.

- The virtual platform symbolizes the new trend in architecture for platform-encompassing frameworks like Java 2 Platform, Enterprise Edition (J2EE™ platform) or Common Object Request Broker Architecture (CORBA).

- Together, all of these form the application.

Systemic qualities of architecture span the differing layers and tiers of a solution. They represent specific characteristics of the solution that the entire system needs to possess. The traits are commonly broken down into five categories, but certainly could include many others. The most common categories are maintainability, manageability, scalability, availability, and securability. These terms are used as follows:

- Maintainability refers to the ability to keep the solution in production through normal maintenance activities like patching and hardware replacement.

- Scalability of a solution allows it to be augmented to handle larger workloads without the need to redesign.

- Manageability refers to the facilities available to conduct the day-to-day administration of the systems.

- Availability allows solutions to remain in continuous service, even in the face of hardware or software faults.

- Securability refers to the solution's capacity to secure data and services from unintended users.

Extracting Requirements From Data

Once you have finished the assessment phase, you need to step back and review the information you have gathered. (When we say finished, we mean finished; do not cheat by beginning to design your architecture before you complete the assessment reports.)

From the mass of data you have compiled, you need to extract information and create assertions about it that become your requirements for the consolidated environment. These assertions should be formally stated, as they create the requirements section of the architecture document.

To illustrate this concept, let's go back to our web server example from Chapter 7. By looking through the data that we gathered there, we might be able to establish the following set of requirements:

TABLE 8-1   Analyzing Data to Generate Requirements

Data Gathered During Assessment	Specific Architectural Requirement
Current solution allows for 24-hour access (except for downtime on third Saturday of each month for 4 hours).	Solution demands 99.95% uptime.
Web traffic allowed from both the Internet and the company's intranet.	Separated network domains and firewalls.
Average 10% concurrence of registered user population (13,000 users) during 1 hour.	Supports 1300 users per hour and up to 1300 sessions.
Database holds approximately 200 GB of user data and needs to be backed up nightly within 4 hour "hot backup" window.	Backup solution capable of sustaining approximately 15 MB/sec required.
No single point of failure within the design.	Load balancing front-end servers and clustering needs to be deployed.

While this is just a brief list of possible requirements, you can see the types of information you need to analyze.

Once you identify requirements from the data gathered during the assessment phase, broadly classify them in the following categories:

- Availability
- Functionality
- Performance
- Management
- Maintenance
- Security

When requirements can be formed for each of the preceding categories, you have probably finished the review. If you cannot draw definitive requirements for any one of the above categories, you need to ask yourself whether this application has a definitive requirement in this area or if you have just failed to gather it.

You might ask why you need to spend so much time reviewing information you spent days, weeks, or even months gathering during the assessment phase. You need to do this for two reasons:

- First, the people who gather information during the assessment phase are very often not the same people who design the solution during the architecture phase. To design an architecture for a consolidated solution that will satisfy specific business needs, you must be intimately familiar with the current environment, its weaknesses, and its potential for consolidation. To obtain this level of familiarity, you must review the information gathered during the assessment phase.

- Second, you don't want to confuse gathering information with analyzing information. The raw data gathered during the assessment phase needs to be turned into information that represents concrete requirements in the form of high- and low-level details, which govern the specification and configuration of the system.

Addressing Common Consolidation Design Issues

Each of the consolidation patterns discussed in Chapter 3 require you to make certain decisions during the architecture phase. Although it is impossible to know all of the decisions that you must make for any particular environment, there are some very common issues to address for each pattern (as addressed in the following sections). In addition, there are problems that are common across all of the patterns. These problems span the common systemic qualities discussed earlier.

The most common issue in designing any consolidated architecture is retaining application isolation in the new environment. All of the questions below relate to this concept of isolation:

- How can you mitigate the risk of all applications and data becoming unavailable if the centralized hardware fails?
- How can you keep one application from affecting other applications or data in the consolidated environment?
- How can you maintain security policies between differing applications?
- How can you separate network communications between applications?

The first concern is fairly easy to address. Reduce the number of failures, limit the effects of failures, and isolate failure to the smallest number of clients. The following techniques and technologies can help you achieve these goals:

- Reducing downtime with redundant hardware
- Isolating failures with domains
- Improving time to recover with Sun Cluster software

Reduce Downtime With Redundant Hardware

The first and most important feature of a highly available consolidated solution is redundant hardware. Components with extra fans, power supplies, disk drives, and even processors can prevent application or data downtime. With most consolidations, you automatically gain additional reliability features when you replace less powerful, older equipment with more robust, newer hardware. For example, redundant power supplies or fans are not typically found on common workgroup PC servers, but almost all enterprise class servers provide these as standard features. More redundant hardware may make your applications or data more available than they were prior to the consolidation.

Isolate Failures

The most important technology that can limit the effects of failure is the concept of domaining. Domaining refers to the specialized hardware and software features of a number of the enterprise class servers offered by Sun. A domain is an electrically isolated server partition within a large chassis that can run its own instance of the Solaris Operating Environment (Solaris OE). From a logical point of view, domains are separate servers. A software error in one server does not affect any other domain on the system. On some servers, redundant hardware is also deployed so that hardware failures do not affect more than one domain on a system. Domains help isolate failure and reduce the risk of application downtime.

Improve Time to Recover With Clustering

You can also reduce the effects of failure on your consolidated environment by using clustering software. There are several implementations and vendors of clustering software, but the basic concept behind them is the same. A redundant server is deployed to take over (known as failover) the duties of the main server in the event of a failure. While failover is not instantaneous, it is usually automatic. Clustering software limits the effects of failure on overall system availability.

Isolating applications to eliminate unwanted resource contention can also be addressed through several means. The method you use to do so depends on the type of workload being executed.

- Managing resource contention in interactive environments
- Managing resource contention in batch environments
- Managing consolidated network communications
- Managing consolidated security concerns

Managing Resource Contention in Interactive Environments

One of the reasons many people consolidate applications onto UNIX, and the Solaris OE in particular, is the increasingly robust resource management available. Within the Solaris OE, there are several ways to control system resource consumption. These methods range from built-in operating environment utilities to dedicated resource managers. We look at the high-level benefits of these options, as well as how they might be used in a consolidated environment. For a more detailed discussion of many of these options, please refer to the Sun BluePrints book, *Resource Management*, by Richard McDougall, Adrian Cockcroft, Evert Hoogendoorn, Enrique Vargas, and Tom Bialaski (ISBN 0-13-025855-5).

The Solaris OE provides a range of built-in tools to control resource management. These tools include the venerable `nice` (and its cousin `renice`) command, scheduler classes, and processor bindings. While these commands are certainly helpful, they are aimed exclusively at CPU resource management and can be somewhat inflexible. Most interactive environments require more robust resource management.

For the Solaris 8 OE and below, Sun offers the Solaris Resource Manager and Solaris Bandwidth Manager products. These products allow you to control certain computing resources (mainly CPU and network bandwidth, respectively) based on certain predefined criteria. In Solaris Resource Manager's case, CPU resources are controlled by the implementation of a "fair share" scheduling class, which prioritizes CPU time between differing user IDs (UIDs) through the use of "shares" that are administrator-defined portions of the resource.

For the Solaris 9 OE and above, the operating environment provides built-in resource management capabilities. This release builds upon the Solaris Resource Manager and Solaris Bandwidth Manager products to cover a greater scope of resources, as well as integrating them better into the operating environment. This section introduces the following new concepts in the Solaris OE's resource management scheme:

- Resource sets expand the roles of processor sets to memory and other resources. Combining these sets, you create a resource pool.

- Pools are special in that they represent not only a logical grouping of resource sets, but also allow you to run processes under different scheduling classes (like fair share or timesharing).

- Projects are network-wide identifiers for related work that run within pools. Typically, these projects are created for individual departments within an organization.

- Tasks are groups of processes doing a single job. They are the lowest level of resource management detail, except individual processes.

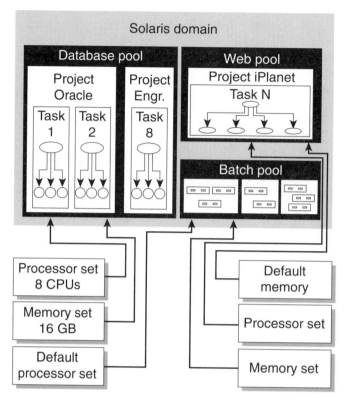

FIGURE 8-2 Putting the Pieces Together

As an example of the integration, processor sets (enhanced to partitions) can be combined with the Solaris 9 Resource Manager to create isolated processing areas. As new versions of Solaris are released, some of these capabilities will be formed into the "containers" paradigm, which allows processes to run within small resource profiles isolated from one another within the same instance of the operating system (OS).

Managing Resource Contention in Batch Environments

Batch processing management is an overlooked area of computer performance in the enterprise computing market. While organizations spend considerable time and effort to optimize their online or interactive processing resources, they neglect the opportunities for using batch processing. Batch processing not only provides more efficient use of resources, but also allows for virtualization of servers through some specialized software called grid engine.

Batch processing resource management is mainly implemented with commercial scheduling packages like Computer Associates's Maestro or BMC's Control-M. These scheduling packages apply complex, branching logic to the running of batch jobs throughout the network. Scheduling packages are a good choice to implement complex batch jobs that depend on particular computing or data resources. For example, many schedulers are deployed to run database reports for corporate accounting systems. This flexibility allows you to stagger the time frames in which certain jobs run on the system.

Grid computing is a step beyond scheduling packages. Grid computing utilizes a similar centralized concept as scheduling packages, but applies computing profiles, user ticketed requests, and policy engines to the overall process. This process results in a more efficient resource utilization and better business alignment. However, the use of grid computing is currently limited to mostly technical computing areas. In the future, look to grid computing to move more into the enterprise mainstream as corporate applications take better advantage of the network's computing resources. Sun provides an open source grid computing solution called grid engine, and it is available at `http://gridengine.sunsource.net/`.

Managing Consolidated Network Communications

Whenever you decide to consolidate multiple servers, storage, or applications together, inevitably you wrestle with the question of how people are going to communicate with the new environment. There are two ways to address this issue:

- Segmented communication channels
- Common communication channels

Segmented communications channels keep the normal communication routes intact by simply moving them to the new environment. For example, if you were consolidating three servers that each had two Ethernet network interfaces (one public "production" interface and another private "management" interface), you would simply duplicate each of these interfaces in the new environment. However, sometimes this approach is not possible (older versions of the Solaris OE require configuration and software to support multiple interfaces on one network segment) or desirable (you don't really need three network interfaces to administer this server). In these cases, we recommend that you create common communication channels for the new environment. In the preceding example, you might keep the three production interfaces to reduce potential client configuration issues and to increase bandwidth, but consolidate the three private interfaces into one.

When we talk about consolidating some interfaces, it is important to properly design the correct amount of functionality into the solutions network communications. At a minimum, account for the following network communications channels:

- Administration
- Production
- Backup

Other channels may be needed, such as monitoring or bulk loading. In addition, many of these channels may need to be redundant through the use of technologies like Internet Protocol Multipathing (IPMP).

Managing Consolidated Security Concerns

Security concerns raised by consolidating servers or storage can be daunting. Many of today's security practices in open-systems architectures are predicated on carefully controlling who can communicate with certain resources by blocking network traffic with firewalls. Sometimes, when you consolidate multiple user communities together, you can destroy the usefulness of these firewalls. In addition, security breaches become more serious due to the fact that several servers might be affected.

While the techniques discussed in the networking section may be helpful in overcoming the first problem (network security and firewalls), you will need to employ some server residence technologies to overcome the second problem. Fortunately, the Solaris OE contains a helpful command called chroot(1M). This command causes any subsequent commands to be executed relative to a supplied root directory. This action isolates any of these commands to a subset of the overall directory. An example of the command is:

```
# /usr/sbin/chroot /opt/jail /opt/apache/bin/httpd
```

This command causes the httpd process to execute as if /opt/jail is its root directory. All system calls will be executed with /opt/jail/ prefixed to the path.

The chroot(1M) command provides a degree of application isolation within the operating system. Because all commands will be directed to a separate directory, you don't have to worry about applications inadvertently overwriting or corrupting other libraries or files. Exploiting this one application only allows access to this subset of the directory structure. In fact, we can further protect this server by limiting the libraries, commands, and configuration files within the chroot environment to only those that the process requires to operate. By doing this, potential intruders will have very limited information and utilities to work with.

Addressing Specific Consolidation Architectures

In the preceding chapters, we discussed several different types of consolidations. The following sections describe solutions to key architectural issues that exist for specific consolidation patterns. These issues include special considerations for:
- Horizontally scaled architectures
- Vertically scaled architectures
- Architectures with centralized databases
- Architectures with consolidated clusters

- Architectures with collapsed tiers
- Architectures that utilize time shifting
- Development, testing, and training environments

Considerations for Horizontally Scaled Architectures

Horizontal scaling generally refers to the addition of servers to handle increasing service loads. This approach is often necessary to address application scalability and availability concerns found in presentation layer services. While increasing the server population seems to contradict the big-picture goal of consolidation, with careful architecture and management, horizontal scaling can actually simplify an environment.

To simplify an environment through horizontal scaling, you can right-size the processing capacity, or you can automate the provisioning and maintenance of these servers.

- **Right-sizing.** When you right-size a server, you ensure that there are no under-utilized processor resources. For example, instead of deploying a redundant set of servers for each of your web applications, have every server run all of the web applications. If you deploy three web applications that all run on an Sun Open Net Environment (Sun ONE) web server, there is no reason to deploy three sets of servers. Unless performance or availability concerns demand it, you just need one set that runs all three applications.

- **Automating provisioning and maintenance.** Another way to simplify your environment when using horizontal scaling is to automate the provisioning and maintenance of the servers. This rational consolidation technique minimizes the differences within the server group so costly administration tasks like patching, installing, and upgrading servers can be automated with technologies like JumpStart™. To enable this strategy, you need to invest, upfront, in software packaging and automation tools.

Make the following considerations when trying to simplify a horizontally scaled environment:

- Consider whether the types of applications you are running play a pivotal role in the ability to utilize either of the preceding strategies. For the most part, only simple, but mature applications support these efforts. Web servers are a prime example of good targets for either, or both, of the preceding strategies.

- Network issues can be paramount to the success of deploying multiple functional applications within the same server set. Consider retaining separate network segments for each application. In this way, you can keep the same Internet Protocol (IP) addresses and host names for the servers, which should cut down on the reconfiguration work for any clients.

- Pay special attention to name space collisions. If your application insists on always looking in the same place for data or configuration information, you might be severely limited in the number of functional instances that you can deploy on a single server.

- Security can be a limiting factor for this type of consolidation, and it is a common obstacle for many consolidations. The key to overcoming this issue in this pattern is to group applications with common users or security profiles.

Horizontal Scaling Example

A good example of how right-sizing and automating maintenance can improve horizontally scaled environments can be seen in web server pools. Many unoptimized environments are configured with a set of three or more web servers serving as a front end to each application. In this scenario, architects do not choose to use three servers to satisfy performance needs, but do so to ensure availability and administration requirements. In addition, installing, provisioning, and administrating these servers are performed manually, one-by-one. Therefore, in an environment of just three or four applications, over a dozen web servers need to be maintained.

A better solution would be to measure the processing load, and deploy an appropriate number of servers to satisfy the need. For the sake of argument, let's say that five servers will satisfy our need. On each of these five servers, one web server is loaded, and the virtual hosts feature is utilized. By equipping each of the servers with a separate network interface (or with two interfaces for highly available network environments), many of the client complexity changes are ignored.

Considerations for Vertically Scaled Architectures

Vertically scalable applications allow you to consolidate multiple servers onto a large server to serve the same user community. Applications that fit into this category tend to be mature or single-purpose applications that exhibit a high degree of scalability. This solution tends to be very implementation-specific (for example, one email application may be very scalable, while another may not).

In the server space, we have the ability to run a single binary architecture, the Solaris OE, across all Sun server and desktop products. The same program will run on any Sun server without porting or other modifications, thus reducing the cost and time required to move applications between servers. The Solaris OE also provides a rich tool set that helps you manage your Sun servers and their various resources. This capability means that it is easier to implement standards and best practices that can leverage scarce IT personnel resources.

To design a vertical scalability consolidation, you need to consider the following issues in addition to the normal architecture:

- **Versions.** Just because a common application has been deployed, it doesn't mean the same application code and patches are in use. In fact, the same vendor might not have even been chosen. A process of harmonizing the application releases should be part of the preliminary work that precedes the implementation of this type of consolidation.

- **Storage.** Concentrating more users on the same server can lead to disk bottlenecks. If this is the case, follow the points under storage consolidations in the following section.

- **Name spaces.** In storage and in the application, it is important that any conflicts in naming are resolved. Oftentimes, this resolution may require some alteration of the client's configurations.

Vertical Scaling Example

Centralizing the file servers for a campus is an example of a vertically scaled consolidation. Network file system (NFS) servers have the ability to scale to dozens of CPUs with near perfect scalability. For this consolidation, we bring together 20 NFS servers from around the campus, and run them on a cluster of larger servers. Making sure that we run through the previous checklist, we arrive at the following solutions:

- All clients and servers are running NFSv3 clients, but the servers have a variety of OS versions (differing NFS implementations). The consolidated servers will be standardized on the last operating environment's NFS implementation.

- Current storage will simply be attached to the file servers through its current mechanisms. This action allows the use of the same volumes. Mount points will be manipulated to prefix the server's current name to the path (for example, `/servername/home/kpepple/`). Client changes will be centrally made in Naming Information Service (NIS).

Considerations for Architectures With Centralized Databases

Centralizing database architectures is another type of vertical scaling; however, it is so important that it deserve special mention. Because all three of the major relational database management systems (RDBMSs) that run on the Solaris OE (Oracle, DB2, and Sybase) vertically scale very well, it is attractive to run many databases on the same server. In addition, most databases are also mature applications with outstanding functionality.

The major architectural decision about centralized database servers is whether to run the databases in multiple, separate instances of the database (one database per instance) or to run them in a single instance. Of course, this decision only affects

RDBMSs that do not distinguish between databases and the instance, most notably Oracle. The benefits and drawbacks to each of the methods for vertically scaling databases are as follows:

- **Multiple-instance databases.** The benefits of implementing multiple-instance databases include the ease of migration and the ease of maintenance multiple instances provide. The drawbacks are that this method does not provide the highest level of total cost of ownership (TCO) savings, generally it requires more memory (for separate copies of the system global area [SGA]), and may not be supported by some independent software vendors (ISVs).

- **Single-instance database.** The benefits of implementing single-instance databases include that it consolidates data in one location, provides a single point of maintenance, and supports a more efficient usage of resources. The drawbacks include the complexity in migration and the potential creation of a single point of failure. Most organizations choose multiple instances for the initial consolidation, and then work on moving them towards a single instance as the application and circumstances allow. If you choose to consolidate to a single instance, we strongly recommend that you deploy clustering software to limit the availability risk.

Another important design choice for this consolidation pattern is the database application you use, and the version of the application. Most organizations want to standardize on a single RDBMS and version during consolidation. While this is not always possible (perhaps due to application dependencies), it is not advisable to mix multiple RDBMSs within the instance of the operating environment. This type of consolidation is rarely supported by ISVs and can lead to problems with shared memory and storage utilization.

Considerations for Architectures With Consolidated Clusters

A lesser-utilized pattern of consolidation is to move from straight one-to-one clustering to N+1 clustering. Basically, this pattern attempts to remove N-1 servers from the environment by vertically scaling the "cold" server to handle the increased load.

Creating this type of consolidation depends heavily on specific implementation details. For example, the clustering solution that is selected will define how large N (the number of servers being clustered) can be, as well as how the failover server needs to be created. Popular solutions for clustering on the Solaris OE include Sun Cluster software and VERITAS Cluster Server.

Some organizations, especially those without disaster recovery capabilities, will find that this method is not a viable option for them. In particular, those applications with downtime costs measured in seconds or minutes are probably not candidates for this type of consolidation. However, for other organizations or applications, this option might be a cost-effective way to increase application availability, while decreasing the number of servers in use.

Considerations for Architectures With Collapsed Tiers

Collapsing architectural tiers simplifies environments by consolidating servers within adjacent architectural tiers. Also, this approach can be employed for applications that feed data to one another. The logic behind this strategy is that the efficiencies gained by reducing communication latency help increase the utilization of computing resources. In addition, this technique reduces the administration burden by decreasing the server population.

When identifying candidates that may benefit from this approach, analyze the application communications and data flows that were documented during the assessment phase. Oftentimes, patterns emerge that point to obvious consolidation opportunities. Keep in mind that you need to weigh these opportunities against the availability and security requirements of applications. For example, although consolidating presentation-tier web servers with their application-tier application servers seems like a perfect match, most organization security policies forbid terminating unknown network connections on servers that contain business logic or data.

Capacity planning is the key to making this consolidation pattern work. While you are increasing efficiency, most of the resource demands will spike higher because usage surges are amplified by the additional workloads. This situation makes the capacity planning exercises in the preceding assessment phase and prototyping later in this phase so important.

Considerations for Architectures That Utilize Time Shifting

Possibly the simplest of the consolidation patterns, time shifting suggests that you schedule processing load when your resources are idle. This method predominately applies to daytime (or work-time) applications combined in the same OS instance as batch jobs that are run overnight.

Most database systems are great candidates for this type of consolidation. During the day, they take care of online transaction processing (OLTP), but after hours they run nightly reporting jobs to be distributed the next morning. To extend this paradigm outside of the database realm, look at the infrastructure required to support work-time computing, including naming servers, Dynamic Host Configuration Protocol (DHCP) servers, authentication servers, network time servers, and monitoring servers. Then, look at the systems that run at night, including backup servers, batch-job servers, and the like.

The opportunities to consolidate resources using this method are substantial. For example, you might consider running the backup server on the same server as the domain naming system (DNS). Perhaps you might consider combining your lightweight directory access protocol (LDAP) server with your NIS server to create a centralized repository for user provisioning.

Several enabling technologies need to be employed to make this consolidation pattern truly feasible. The first is an intelligent job scheduler. Beyond the simple cron utility, this tool schedules jobs with branching logic and tracks the results. The second technology you should employ is a resource manager. Just because you don't use the DNS services as heavily during the nighttime hours as you do during the day, it doesn't mean you don't use them at all.

Considerations for Development, Testing, and Training Environments

Most of the consolidation techniques deployed in the production environment should be deployed in the development, testing, and training environments as well. Because these environments are some of the greatest contributors to server sprawl, you should attack them with equal vigor. In fact, many people contend that if you consolidate the production environment, you have to match the development, testing, and training environments to it.

While a technical resource management package is essential to successfully extending consolidation strategies to these environments, diplomacy and scheduling are the most important factors to making them work. Getting development, testing, and training personnel to coordinate times when they might need nearly exclusive access to a machine can be difficult, to say the least. However, if you are consolidating the production environment, the experience should lead to better solutions being deployed.

Sizing the Consolidated Architecture

Once you have decided on the acceptable consolidation targets for your project, you need to spend some time sizing the resource required to host it. Revisiting the performance monitoring information from the assessment phase, remember that capacity planning involves the following activities:

- Establishing a performance baseline
- Defining the system's peak utilization period
- Constructing a performance model of the system from the peak period utilization data
- Projecting future utilizations after system configuration changes

The first two steps are addressed during the assessment phase; therefore, the following sections concentrate on the final two steps of the process.

Construct a System Performance Model

Once you identify the peak utilization period, extract the performance data and system hardware configuration for that time interval, and input it into the system model. In such a model, each resource in the system (every CPU, controller, disk drive, and network adapter) is treated as a queue, and the system is viewed as a network of these queues. The measured performance data is used to calibrate the model. The model itself defines the system in mathematical terms. When calibrated, the model represents the baseline as it existed when the data was collected.

There are several ways to create a system model. By far the easiest way is to use packaged software tools like BMC's Best/1 Predict or TeamQuest's Model. Both of these tools are part of larger performance management suites, which can also be used for monitoring server performance. In this chapter, we use TeamQuest's Model software for our example.

There are several steps to creating your system model in TeamQuest's software:
- Build the model.
- Adjust the model.
- Calibrate the model.
- Merge models.
- Predict effects of change on the model.

The first step in creating your system model is to build the model with TeamQuest's Model Builder Wizard. The wizard steps you through the process of importing the model input file you created during the assessment phase (see "Estimating Utilization" on page 95) into the TeamQuest Model tool. It reads the information about your server's configuration, resource utilization, and workloads to create a queueing model that describes your server's performance. Most of the time, this step consists of nothing more than locating your model input file (that you backed up during the assessment phase), and letting the wizard create the model. However, sometimes the wizard may need help identifying certain hardware resources. This is most often the case when you have a new server with recent processors or disks. If this is the case, TeamQuest will present a window asking you to select a similar resource, or define a new one.

Once the model is created, adjust it to make sure that it accurately reflects the modeled server. This change may involve adjusting active resources (resources that perform units of work like a processor or disk drive), adding passive resources (like memory), adjusting I/O measurements, and consolidating non essential workloads.

Of the many adjustments that you can make, the most important is the I/O measurement adjustment. Modern I/O resources, like Sun StorEdge 9960 arrays, are very complex to model effectively in any tool.

With the model created and adjusted to your liking, it is time to calibrate the model. Calibrating the model compares it against the measured results (from your model input file). If the results are not within a certain tolerance, the tool adjusts the model before repeating the process. This usually continues until the model falls within tolerances. Luckily, TeamQuest Model automates this process so that you only need to state the tolerance level (usually 1 percent) and then it will do the rest.

Usually, the model calibrates itself within a few minutes. However, on large servers with many disks or workloads this can take a substantial amount of time. If you have a server that fits in this classification, make sure that you run TeamQuest Model on a fast computer.

Once the model is calibrated, you are ready to start performing capacity planning exercises; however, if you are consolidating multiple applications into a single instance of the operating system, you have an extra step to consider. TeamQuest Model has a unique feature that merges the workloads from one model into another model. Before using that feature, make sure that both models have the same system type. If they do not, change one of the models into the other's system type with the Change To Different System Type command. The four-step window that appears shows the current system type and configuration, and asks you to choose the new system type, CPU name, CPU count, and relative performance. This process is relatively easy, with the exception of the relative performance.

The nonzero number describes the new system's performance compared to current systems. This can be estimated by comparing Transaction Performance Processing Council (TPC-C) or Standard Performance Evaluation Corporation (SPECint) ratings for the machines, depending on whether it is a database server or general computation machine. You do not have to limit either of these ratings, but they are a good place to start. You can find TPC-C ratings at http://www.tpc.org and SPECint scores at http://www.spec.org. Of course, if you are consolidating Solaris OE to Solaris OE servers, you can skip this step.

With the models both sharing the same system type, you can merge the models together. Simply open one model in the tool, then choose the File > Merge Models command to choose the other model you wish to merge. Once the two models are merged, you will have one CPU active resource, but all the disk resources from both models. In addition, all of the workloads from both models will be represented in the merged model. Go through the model and delete the workloads and redundant active resources from the model so that it more clearly represents your proposed consolidation. You might want to add or change the CPU resources to better match your proposal (you can always change those types of variables once you start the prediction step of the process). Repeat these steps (including the changing system type steps) for the model that you want to consolidate. Once the models have been merged, do not recalibrate the model.

Project Changes in the Model

With the baseline model completed, you can project changes into the model to see how utilization might change if you add additional workloads. Also, you can see how changing the underlying server platform affects performance (modify the system hardware configuration to determine the effect). This change can include adding CPUs, increasing CPU speed, adding I/O controllers or changing their performance characteristics, adding disk drives, and changing redundant area of independent disks (RAID) characteristics. In addition, you can combine workloads from different systems on a single system to see how they might perform together.

System modeling is a powerful tool for capacity and performance planning, allowing you to explore any number of workload intensities and system configurations in advance of system utilization growth and equipment deployment. System modeling can also provide workload metrics needed to establish and maintain Service Level Agreements at the application and system level.

Once workload combinations have been finalized, prioritize them. This information will be used during the specification and deployment to configure the appropriate resource management schemes. You do not need to include a great level of detail in the prioritization during this phase; however, you should include both an ordered ranking and an approximate percentage of the machine it will require. Approximate the percentage from the earlier high-level sizing exercises, and don't worry if your estimate seems inaccurate, because you will tweak and refine it during the deployment, testing, and production of the solution.

Now that the model has been created, adjusted, calibrated, and merged, you can use the tool to predict the effects of workloads or resources on the performance of the consolidated environment. The software allows you to modify a large number of variables about the system model. You can change the CPU resources (speed, number or type), disk resources, workload intensities, or even memory size.

For the purposes of this exercise, solve the model to find out what the effect of consolidating the workloads has on the server's performance. To do that, choose the Predict > MVAP Solver option from the TeamQuest Model menus. The resulting window allows you to specify what parts of the model that you can predict from. Because this example does not model the workload growth, choose the Solve Single Step option and leave the rest of the options unchecked.

The software solves the model, accounting for the newly defined workloads on the active resources. As a result, it shows the solved model with the statistics for the single step chosen earlier.

You can export the results of this modeling to StarOffice™ software for visualization by following the instructions in the white paper available at http://www.teamquest.com/html/products/wpapers.shtml. This step is invaluable for understanding how you may have to change your model to deliver on your service levels for the consolidation.

Prototyping the Initial Solution

Prototyping is the next step in completing the consolidation architecture. When you prototype a solution, you create a scaled-down version of the proposed architecture, and experiment with it to prove that the assumptions made during the previous phase can be supported when they are implemented. Prototyping enables you to identify the obvious (and sometimes not so obvious) problems that may arise when you consolidate applications, storage, and servers. This task can greatly reduce the amount of time you spend during the implementation phase.

Most of the problems you identify during prototyping fall under the common testing categories of function, performance, or integrity. However, the difficult goal, here, is to test harmony. You already know that the applications work because they are running in production, so the bulk of the work during this task involves looking for corner cases that break the consolidation.

Building the Prototype

To prototype the consolidation, you need to build a consolidated solution. Ideally, you will do this on a server or on an array sized to the general specifications of the results of the capacity planning exercise detailed in "Sizing the Consolidated Architecture" on page 124. Unfortunately, it is rare that you will have that much spare hardware sitting idle. Luckily, in this phase, you only need to validate the concept; you don't need to prove that the implementation is completely correct. As such, you can scale down the hardware requirements, as long as you ensure that you use similar characteristics.

For example, if your sizing calls for a fully loaded Sun Fire 15K server split into four domains running the Solaris 8 OE, you can probably make do with a Sun Fire 6800 server with four domains running the Solaris 8 OE. What's important is that you keep the same number of domains and the same OE. The same is true for storage. It might be useful to model a Sun StorEdge 9960 array across a fully redundant storage area network (SAN) fabric with a single SAN switch on a Sun StorEdge 9910 array. Again, the main points are the SAN switch and the StorEdge array family. The same concept holds true for application and RDBMS data. The binaries and schema are important, but the full bulk of the data is not as important. Make sure that the exact versions of software that are being tested in the prototype are the same versions that you will deploy in production.

Testing the Prototype

Once the infrastructure is built for the prototype, you need to test the prototype. Testing should cover the following areas:

- **Configuration.** Does everything install correctly? Are there any namespace, driver, or library issues? Does the installation need to be changed?
- **Functionality.** Do all the applications work as they are supposed to?
- **Integrity.** Are the data produced by the applications correct?
- **Performance.** Do the applications perform as they did before the consolidation? Will the architecture scale to meet the requirements?
- **Operations.** Can the solution be backed up and restored? Can the solution be monitored and administered?

Of course, you need to conduct this testing in a controlled environment, free from the production network and servers. Although the testing for each prototype will differ, these types of testing should be covered for all of them.

It may make sense to put some effort into automating some of these tests with commercial packages or custom written scripts. Tests that are important to run during the prototyping phase become critical during the actual migration. Creating an automated test could save countless hours during the migration and avoid downtime once the new environment is put into production. As a rule of thumb, automate testing when you anticipate more than five repetitions or more than two hours of testing.

Revising the Solution

Once the results are back from the prototyping phase, it is time to evaluate the results, measure requirements against the results, and fix anything that doesn't measure up. Think of this as the time after the qualifying runs at a car race, but before the actual race. It is time to tune up our architecture to ensure that everything works and is in tip-top shape when it comes time to migrate and deploy the solution.

This revision is necessary due to one inescapable truth of consolidation: Nothing ever works entirely right the first time. Consolidation is a delicate balance of resources and utilization, which can be very difficult to perfect anywhere but in the real world. Because the prototyping exercise is the closest you can come to the "real world" of production, it is where you draw the best data. To evaluate the results of the prototyping exercise, categorize your test results into three categories: pass, marginal pass, and fail.

Begin by looking at the tests that fail. These are obvious problems that you need to fix. They are also the areas where the architecture will change the most. Oftentimes, a critical decision in the architecture needs to be completely replaced with a different technology. While you are looking at failed tests, keep an eye on the marginal tests. Oftentimes, some of the marginal tests point to a similar decision or technology used in the failed test.

Marginal tests are the most difficult to gauge. They might mean something significant, or they might only expose a limitation of the scaled-down software and hardware where you are testing the prototype. The key is to focus on the details to see if any of the other tests point to a similar result. Corroboration is cause for further investigation. Otherwise, document the marginal results, and through the implementation phase, look for other signs that the test is something other than a simple diversion.

Documenting the Solution

When you are finally done evaluating the prototyping tests, the consolidated architecture is ready to be implemented. However, before you begin the implementation phase, it is very important to document the architecture and the prototyping tests that got you to this point.

You need to document this step for many of the same reasons that you document extensively in the other phases of the project. Because this is probably only one consolidation in the context of a much larger project, a documented architecture aids in repeatability. Just as the consolidation patterns presented in this book help you create known-good architectures, this step starts the creation of your own set of consolidation patterns. These can then be shared and copied in other parts of your organization for future consolidations. In addition, these documents serve as a template for other unrelated consolidations.

The easiest way to document the solution is to create an architecture document. This document contains the following information:

- **Requirements.** Restate the requirements gathered in the assessment phase.
- **Architecture.** Outline the architecture divided into logical and physical components, with functional data flow charts and logical application layouts, and document the sizing output.
- **Prototype.** Document the hardware and software configuration of the prototype environment. Sun often uses the Explorer tool to automate this step.
- **Test.** Document the tests and their results, as well as any remedial design changes.

Summary

This chapter explained how to perform the tasks involved in designing a consolidated architecture. These tasks include reviewing requirements, developing an initial solution, prototyping the design, revising the design, and documenting the architecture.

## CHAPTER 9

Implementing a Consolidated Solution

After you finish the assessment, create the architecture, and prototype the architecture, it's time to implement the solution. You need to specify the low-level details of the platform, define a migration strategy, build the consolidated environment, and deploy it. Before you put the solution into production, ensure that the administrative staff is trained, and be prepared to document the results of the consolidation. It may seem like a lot to do, but if you have done the due diligence during the assessment and architecture phases, this should be the easiest step to complete.

This chapter provides information about performing the following tasks:

- "Preparing for the Consolidation" on page 133
- "Implementing the Consolidation" on page 145

Preparing for the Consolidation

With the documentation from the architecture phase in hand, it is time to detail how you will implement the consolidated solution. Capture this information in a document called a build specification, which serves as a blueprint to follow as you build a solution.

From a high level, the implementation planning process consists of the following steps:
- Creating a build specification
- Building the environment
- Defining your migration strategy
- Practicing the consolidation
- Backing up the old environments

Creating a Build Specification

Build specifications differ depending on the kind of consolidation you are pursuing, as well as what you are implementing to facilitate the consolidation. Data center consolidations may need a complete specification of the space, power, and environmentals, while a simple re-hosting of several applications on newer platforms might only require a server specification. Whatever your goal, build specifications are the authoritative document for installers to use to answer almost any question during an implementation or migration. Build specifications define the information gathered and recorded during the assessment phase.

Some special things need to be addressed in the build specification of consolidated servers:

- Application file layouts of binaries for all applications
- Resource management configurations
- Fault isolation configurations

Remember that this document is the exact blueprint of the system to be installed. Don't leave anything out or to the imagination. Even if you will be doing the installation yourself, you should create this document with the thought in mind that you will have an outside vendor implement it.

Building the Environment

The first step in migrating to the consolidated environment is to build the target environment. Armed with a build specification, you are ready to deploy the hardware and software infrastructure, so that everything is ready when you need to move the production data. Up to this point, you have concentrated on working with a top-down design; however, when you build the consolidated environment, you need to build from the bottom up. This task includes the following subtasks:

- Preparing the physical environment
- Installing the arrays and servers
- Installing the software infrastructure
- Installing the application software
- Identifying temporary hardware requirements

Prepare the Physical Environment

Before you can implement the consolidated solution, the data center infrastructure needs to be completely ready as planned during the architecture phase. In addition to the planned elements like floor plan, electricity, cooling, and cabling, some procedural elements need to be worked through. Most important are ingress routing and temporary equipment floor space.

Just because you have space available for the new server or storage, there is no guarantee that you can get it to the new location. Carefully plan the route all the way from the docks, or building entry way, to the assigned floor space, paying close attention to the size and weight restrictions of the environment. All floors, doorways, hallways, and elevators need to be large enough, and strong enough, for the equipment to arrive at its assigned area. It is not uncommon to have to apply heroic measures to permit the ingress of new equipment. These efforts may include hiring cranes, removing walls, and creating new doorways. While these factors may not kill your project, they certainly may delay it.

In addition to the ingress route, leave a buffer space around the new equipment. You may want to physically locate some of the consolidated servers near the new equipment to facilitate creative data transfer techniques with private IP networking and storage area networks. In this space, ensure that you have access to extra cables to make these connections, if needed.

Install Arrays and Servers

At this point, the hardware should be physically installed in the area you prepared in the data center. If you are doing an application and storage consolidation, it is time to install the storage arrays and servers. Ideally, put the storage in place first. It is always beneficial to have spare storage space available when installing, consolidating, or migrating systems.

As part of the installation, make sure that the arrays or servers are thoroughly tested and burned in. Catching problems up-front in this phase can save an immense amount of time during the actual consolidation.

This is also a great time to make sure that the backup solution is in place. You will need to back up the old and new environments several times during the actual migration. We have seen that migrations go smoother, and servers go into production faster, with a backup solution in place.

Install the Software Infrastructure

With the data center properly configured and the servers or arrays in place, it is time to start laying the software infrastructure. The software infrastructure is all the software necessary to operate and manage the server or array, except for the actual application and data. This infrastructure might consist of the following components:
- The operating environment
- A volume manager
- Monitoring tools and agents
- Backup software

Again, the installation and configuration of this software should already have been defined in the build specification created earlier. Although your initial inclination might be to simply restore a backup of the consolidated server instead of installing from scratch, resist it. We have found that reinstalling from scratch saves time and provides a more stable base in the long run.

At this time, decide whether to install the servers manually or through an automated fashion (such as using JumpStart software). For most consolidations, the benefits of creating an automated JumpStart server far exceed the time and effort required to install it. This is especially apparent when you consider the possibility of installing some servers or domains several times during the course of migration practice and testing. For information about using JumpStart servers in automated installations, refer to *JumpStart Technology: Effective Use in the Solaris Operating Environment*, by John Howard and Alex Noordergraaf (ISBN 0-13-062154-4).

After loading the operating environment and infrastructure software, thoroughly test it to make sure that it provides a strong foundation for the applications. If backup software and hardware are in place, this is a good time to back up the solution foundation. You might end up needing to reinstall or recover the environment as a result of your application testing during practice migrations.

Install the Application Software

Now, it is time to actually install the applications. Install and configure the first one as you normally would, using configuration files from the old system as a guide. Again, resist the temptation to simply insert the old configuration files into the system. Invariably, something in the new setup has changed that creates a very subtle performance or availability problem that you will need to debug.

Make sure to pay close attention to your build specification during installations. To enable many resource management facilities, you need to install applications to run under special user accounts. In addition, watch the installation directories for data and binaries. These points are especially important when you are installing several instances of the same application, because they usually default to the same directory structures and owners. Failing to carefully follow your build specification may result in having to reinstall your application(s).

Before you move to the subsequent applications, take time to install the application in the chroot environment if that has been called for in the design.

▼ To Create a `chroot` Environment:

1. Test the software and make sure that it works properly and turn on the system trace functionality for the application to trap any `open(2)` system calls with a command similar to the following:

```
#truss -f -o testfile -t open httpd
```

This command captures all of the library and file opening calls of the process (and its children with the `-f` option) to ensure they are moved into the `chroot` environment later. The output from the `truss` command in the test file should appear similar to the following:

```
# more /tmp/testfile
1015:   open("/var/ld/ld.config", O_RDONLY)                   Err#2 ENOENT
1015:   open("/usr/ucblib/libpam.so.1", O_RDONLY)             Err#2 ENOENT
1015:   open("/usr/lib/libpam.so.1", O_RDONLY)                = 3
1015:   open("/usr/ucblib/libdl.so.1", O_RDONLY)              Err#2 ENOENT
1015:   open("/usr/lib/libdl.so.1", O_RDONLY)                 = 3
1015:   open("/usr/ucblib/libresolv.so.2", O_RDONLY)          Err#2 ENOENT
1015:   open("/usr/lib/libresolv.so.2", O_RDONLY)             = 3
1015:   open("/usr/ucblib/libm.so.1", O_RDONLY)               Err#2 ENOENT
1015:   open("/usr/lib/libm.so.1", O_RDONLY)                  = 3
1015:   open("/usr/ucblib/libcrypt_i.so.1", O_RDONLY)         Err#2 ENOENT
1015:   open("/usr/lib/libcrypt_i.so.1", O_RDONLY)            = 3
1015:   open("/usr/ucblib/libsocket.so.1", O_RDONLY)          Err#2 ENOENT
1015:   open("/usr/lib/libsocket.so.1", O_RDONLY)             = 3
1015:   open("/usr/ucblib/libnsl.so.1", O_RDONLY)             Err#2 ENOENT
1015:   open("/usr/lib/libnsl.so.1", O_RDONLY)                = 3
1015:   open("/usr/ucblib/libc.so.1", O_RDONLY)               Err#2 ENOENT
1015:   open("/usr/lib/libc.so.1", O_RDONLY)                  = 3
1015:   open("/usr/lib/libgen.so.1", O_RDONLY)                = 3
1015:   open("/usr/lib/libmp.so.2", O_RDONLY)                 = 3
1015:   open("/usr/platform/SUNW,Ultra-2/lib/libc_psr.so.1",O_RDONLY) = 3
1015:   open("/opt/local/apache-1.3.12/conf/httpd.conf", O_RDONLY) = 3
1015:   open64("/etc/.name_service_door", O_RDONLY)      = 4
1015:   open("/opt/local/apache-1.3.12/conf/srm.conf", O_RDONLY) = 3
1015:   open("/opt/local/apache-1.3.12/conf/access.conf", O_RDONLY) = 3
```

The important lines within this file are those that have a positive return value (they assigned a file descriptor to the `open(2)` command). Libraries within this output can usually be identified by a `lib` file path or file name in the form of `libraryname.so.X`. To quickly find these `open(2)` calls, you can use a command similar to the following:

```
# grep -v Err /tmp/testfile | grep lib | cut -d" " -f1 | cut -f2 | sort -u
open("/usr/lib/libc.so.1",
open("/usr/lib/libcrypt_i.so.1",
open("/usr/lib/libdl.so.1",
open("/usr/lib/libgen.so.1",
open("/usr/lib/libm.so.1",
open("/usr/lib/libmp.so.2",
open("/usr/lib/libnsl.so.1",
open("/usr/lib/libpam.so.1",
open("/usr/lib/libresolv.so.2",
open("/usr/lib/libsocket.so.1",
open("/usr/lib/locale/en_US.ISO8859-1/en_US.ISO8859-1.so.2",
open("/usr/lib/nss_files.so.1",
open("/usr/lib/nss_nis.so.1",
open("/usr/platform/SUNW,Ultra-2/lib/libc_psr.so.1",
open("/usr/share/lib/zoneinfo/US/Pacific",
#
```

Realize that this is an inexact way to identify the libraries needed. You will have to do further testing and experimentation to create a complete list.

The `ldd(1)` utility provides an easier way to map all the library dependencies, but you will still need to `truss(1)` to trap any `open(2)` calls for configuration and data files. The `ldd(1)` utility is invoked with the following command:

```
# ldd httpd
        libaprutil.so.0 =>        /opt/apache/lib/libaprutil.so.0
        libexpat.so.0 =>          /opt/apache/lib/libexpat.so.0
        libapr.so.0 =>    /opt/apache/lib/libapr.so.0
        libsendfile.so.1 =>       /usr/lib/libsendfile.so.1
        librt.so.1 =>    /usr/lib/librt.so.1
        libm.so.1 =>    /usr/lib/libm.so.1
        libsocket.so.1 =>         /usr/lib/libsocket.so.1
        libnsl.so.1 =>    /usr/lib/libnsl.so.1
        libresolv.so.2 =>         /usr/lib/libresolv.so.2
        libdl.so.1 =>    /usr/lib/libdl.so.1
        libpthread.so.1 =>        /usr/lib/libpthread.so.1
        libc.so.1 =>    /usr/lib/libc.so.1
        libaio.so.1 =>    /usr/lib/libaio.so.1
        libmd5.so.1 =>    /usr/lib/libmd5.so.1
        libmp.so.2 =>    /usr/lib/libmp.so.2
        libthread.so.1 =>         /usr/lib/libthread.so.1
        /usr/platform/SUNW,Ultra-2/lib/libc_psr.so.1
        /usr/platform/SUNW,Ultra-2/lib/libmd5_psr.so.1
#
```

These files need to be accessible under the `chroot` environment. In this example, we need to ensure that the `/usr/lib` libraries, `/usr/platform` library, and apache configuration files are moved to the `chroot` environment.

2. **Create the `chroot` environment for the application. This involves creating directory structures, copying libraries, and minimizing some vital configuration files.**

   ■ At a minimum, create the basic file system with `etc`, `etc/default`, `dev`, `usr`, `usr/bin`, `usr/lib`, `usr/lib/security`, `usr/share`, and `usr/share/lib`. Usually, you can create symbolic links for the `bin` directory (linking it to `usr/bin` and the `lib` directory) to `usr/lib`.

   ■ The application needs to access some of the system libraries; the hard part is finding out which libraries need to be accessed. The output of the preceding file (`testfile`) should provide some answers. Look through it for all the libraries opened (`*.so` files) in the output, and copy these files to the appropriate directory within the `chroot` environment.

- Basic configuration files like passwd and nsswitch also need to reside in the chroot environment. Again, the output from the truss command should help you determine which configuration files are needed for the application. As a usual set on minimal files, start with:

  etc/default/init

  etc/netconfig

  etc/pam.conf

  usr/bin/ls

  /etc/passwd

  /etc/shadow

  /etc/group

  /etc/hosts

  /etc/nsswitch.conf

- You will also need to create some device files. A minimal set would usually include:

  dev/conslog

  dev/null

  dev/tcp

  dev/ticlts

  dev/ticots

  dev/ticotsord

  dev/tty

  dev/udp

  dev/zero

  a. To create these files, you will need to use the mknod(1M) command. As part of that command, you will need to learn the major and minor numbers for your current devices. You can find this out with the following command:

```
# ls -1L /dev/null | awk '{print substr($1,1,1), $5, $6}' \ | sed -e s/,//
c 13 2
#
```

b. With the output of that command ("c 13 2" in the example), you can create your /dev/null device with the following invocation of the mknod command:

```
# mknod null c 13 2
```

   c. Repeat this for all of the devices that you might need to create.

3. Make sure the partition is mounted with the setuid option.

4. Move the entire installed software tree to the same place within the chroot environment. The software tree must have the same path under the chroot environment as it did under the regular operating system. Make sure you actually copy or move the files here; links defeat the purpose of this exercise and often don't work.

5. Manually start the application in the chroot environment. Change /chrootdir/ to the directory you have chosen to create your chroot environment. To invoke the application, use the form:

```
# /usr/sbin/chroot /chrootdir /opt/apache/bin/httpd
```

6. Using this command changes the root to /chrootdir/ and starts the httpd daemon within the chroot environment. Thoroughly test that the application works correctly.

7. Modify the application's startup script to include the chroot invocation that you used in the preceding step. The startup script usually resides in the /etc/init.d/ directory.

8. Sanitize the system configuration files to remove any unnecessary information. The less information that is available in these files, the less information that might be available to potential hackers.

Only keep entries needed for the operation of these processes in these files. Note that this allows the chroot environment to keep different configuration files than those used in the regular operating environment (for example, the non-chroot environment).

9. Test, test, test. While you will formally test the application later, it doesn't hurt to catch some of the problems now. This might save a lot of time later, especially if it means that you are not replicating errors in other installations.

10. With the first application in place, repeat this process until all of the applications are in place on the system.

11. **As you install and configure each application, have the previously installed applications up and running. This gives you a good feel for the potential impact of the new application, as well as exposure to maintaining multiple applications within one instance of the operating system.**

Identify Temporary Hardware Requirements

With all the applications in place, running, and tested, you are almost done building the consolidated environment. The only thing remaining is to determine whether any special migration or conversion hardware support is needed. This may include spare scratch storage area, special network cables, or even specialized expansion cards (such as mainframe channel attachment units). If they are required as part of the data migration process, this is a good time to put them into the environment.

For most consolidations, we recommend setting aside quite a bit of extra storage space for the migration. We usually set aside three times the current binary space and five times the current data space, as follows:
- One copy of the installed binary
- One copy of the chroot copy of binaries
- One copy of the install packages
- Two copies of the data for practice migrations
- One copy of the data for backup
- One copy of the consolidated data
- One copy of the production data

Obviously, some migration might need quite a bit more space to complete.

Defining a Data Migration Strategy

While you familiarize yourself and your staff with the new environment, create a data migration strategy. This strategy should explain the process for moving application data from the old machine to the new environment, with complete integrity and speed. It should also address how you can reverse this procedure if something goes wrong. Data migration strategies range from very simplistic to incredibly complex.

Simple data migrations are usually found in environments with either small data sets or with long downtime windows. For most nondatabase applications, data simply resides in files on the operating system that need to be copied to the new machine. Most often, this is done with the help of network file system (NFS), but other types of transport like File Transfer Protocol (FTP) or tape backups can be effective.

Complex data migrations usually result from very small downtime windows or extremely large data sets. These tend to be very specific to the application, because they involve some kind of specialized data migration technique. Sometimes this can be built into the application (in the case of replication server technology), but most often, you need to utilize specialized data management software like Instant Image.

Database applications are the most difficult to migrate, because they may not reside on an actual file system (raw partition), and may have special characteristics. The following sections describe the special options for database data migrations.

Relational database data migrations are in a class by themselves. For the reasons just mentioned, they need specialized data migration techniques. For the examples in this section, we use an Oracle relational database management systems (RDBMSs). Other databases have similar options. With Oracle, you have the following three major options for migrating data into a consolidated environment. Each has advantages and disadvantages that make it more suitable for some applications than for others.

- **Export/Import.** Using this option, you export a database out of one instance and import it into the new consolidated environment. This is the most flexible migration, but can be very complex, especially for inexperienced database administrators. This is often the choice of Oracle-to-Oracle consolidations across platforms, operating systems, or versions.

- **COPY statement.** Using SQL, you can copy data from one database to another. This is rarely used, as it requires the same versions of Oracle and the operating system.

- **Oracle Database Workbench.** This tool was created to facilitate migrations to Oracle from other RDBMSs. With a wizard-driven, graphical user interface, it helps convert data from other database systems for insertion into a new Oracle database. This is a great help for organizations moving from one database vendor to Oracle, but is limited to databases that Oracle supports. Currently, these include DB2, MS SQL, Sybase, Informix and MySQL. This tool runs under Microsoft Windows and Linux.

Whatever migration strategy you choose, work out the details through practice runs of the actual migration. This process is best done with the sandbox, or test, environment that you set aside earlier, and a replica of either the old servers or arrays. This method allows the experimentation required to create not only a serviceable migration, but an optimal one. Crucial pieces of the experimentation include time and utilization monitors. This might be the same software used during the assessment phase (for example, TeamQuest). Be sure to time and monitor each practice migration run so you can objectively compare each run against the others. When you finally have a process in place that works well, make sure to document all the steps, as well as the configuration files.

Create a Back-Out Process

After the migration process has been documented, create a back-out process that details the steps required to put the old environment back into production in case problems arise at any step within the migration procedure. In the back-out process, state the criteria for backing out of the migration. This information usually revolves around two factors, time and functionality.

Practicing the Consolidation

With the easy foundation installations out of the way, the consolidation gets a little more difficult. Now, it is time to migrate or consolidate application data. However, before jumping into that process, practice it several times so you know exactly what to do and how to do it. When it comes time move the data, you will be under time constraints to get the applications back in service. We recommend that you practice the migration at least three times after you have successfully completed it within your time and availability requirements, to establish a valid timing measurement.

Become Familiar With the New Environment

The first part to practicing the consolidation is to get your staff familiar with the new environment and applications. Many times during a consolidation, foreign hardware and new versions of software are deployed. This may be a large multidomained Sun Fire 15K server, a new version of the operating environment (like Solaris 9), or both. Whatever your consolidation entails, you need to ensure that the people migrating the data and administering the new environment are able to competently do their jobs, and to take advantage of new features.

The easiest way to familiarize everyone with the new environment is to set aside some time and capacity (storage volumes or domains) as a sandbox, or test, area. In the part of the machine you set aside for practice runs, people can use the storage or server to learn about its operation and capabilities. In addition, practicing in a test environment provides confidence for inexperienced staff members. Note that this practice doesn't replace the need for training (discussed later in this chapter) rather it augments the training.

Backing Up Old Environments

After building the consolidated environment and practicing the consolidation, schedule a full, cold backup of the environment. Schedule this backup as close to the migration date as possible. This backup is the heart of many back-out procedures.

Equally important to backing up the old environment is actually testing that the backup is valid. While this important testing function is skipped in most production data centers, it is imperative here. It is hard to tell what impact your migration may have on your data, so take the extra time and restore the entire backup on a test system. In addition to testing your backup's integrity, it also provides valuable peace of mind. As my first boss once told me, "the job you save may be your own."

Implementing the Consolidation

When you have finished the contingency planning and documented your practice migrations to your satisfaction, the time of reckoning is upon you. It is now time to actually migrate the applications or data to the new environment, and move them into production. Most consolidations require the following steps to implement their consolidation:

- Migrating applications
- Testing the configuration
- Tuning the configuration
- Documenting the results of the configuration
- Training the administrative staff

The time and complexity that these steps represent vary depending on your application.

Migrating Applications

After completing the background work, all that is left to do is to execute the consolidation plans. Before you start, make sure that you have scheduled the appropriate technical and business teams. Because most consolidations take place during nonbusiness hours, it is important to get everyone involved before you begin. In addition, it might be a good time to coordinate activity on the network before the migration. Other large jobs and transfers should be deferred for the migration period. In addition, just as in the practice runs, monitoring should be in place for the migration.

With those prerequisites completed, you are ready to begin following the migration procedures. If you have properly prepared, and luck is on your side, this entire step should be anticlimactic; however, watch the monitoring software during the migration to be sure no problems arise, and investigate abnormalities if they appear.

Testing the Consolidation

Testing the consolidation takes a lot of time. It is not unusual for testing to take four times as long as the migration of data. Testing should include the following tests:

- Functional tests
- Performance tests
- Backup tests
- Data and application correctness tests

Tuning the Configuration

After the data migration, and conversion and testing are complete, it is time to spend a few minutes tuning the system before moving the new consolidated system into production. Tuning the new environment will consist of two major steps:

- Final performance tuning
- Applying resource management

The final performance tuning looks to add modifications to enhance the server's configuration and performance to the new applications. Typically, this will include:

- Adjusting the shared memory settings
- Balancing I/O settings
- Modifying network settings
- Setting dump sizes and locations

While the individual tuning actions will vary from one server to another, it is important that each of these changes are tested and documented.

There are three steps in applying resource management to your newly consolidated server. They are:

- Categorizing
- Controlling
- Accounting

Categorizing your projects is very similar to the workload creation that you performed with TeamQuest during the assessment phase of the consolidation. In fact, you might be able to use the same raw data in the section (assuming that the configuration and workloads haven't changed too much). However, this factor is very dependent on the version of the Solaris OE that you are using. Many of the concepts of categorizing workloads were introduced in the Solaris 8 OE update 1 and the Solaris 9 OE.

The highest level of workload categorization is projects. Projects allow you to create administrative distinctions or groupings between applications. Most organizations will use projects to denote divisions, departments, or initiatives. To create a project, you use the projadd(1M) command. The results are usually recorded in the /etc/projects file. However, you can opt to use a network-wide repository such as LDAP instead of this flat file.

```
# projadd -c "ecommerce project" -U 60001 -p 202 ecommerce
# cat /etc/project
system:0::::
user.root:1::::
noproject:2::::
default:3::::
group.staff:10::::
ken:201:test project:40619::
ecommerce:202:ecommerce project:60001::
```

The -u argument adds the user ID 60001 (the nobody user) to this project.

Below the project level, commands and shell scripts execute as tasks. The newtask(1) command allows users to assign processes and commands to different projects. This assignment allows users, who might be participants in more than one project, to differentiate their work. The following would be an example of a user assigning their command to the e-commerce project:

```
# newtask -p ecommerce /opt/apache/bin/httpd
```

These tasks can also be performed graphically using the Sun Management Console, as you will see in the next section.

Controlling your consolidated environment is more difficult than categorizing it. This calls for applying restraints to the consumption of resources by projects, tasks, or processes within the operating environment. This is primarily accomplished by using features of Solaris Resource Manager software or the Solaris 9 Resource Manager software. We will illustrate the concept with the Solaris 9 Resource Manager software and the Sun Management Console. From within Sun Management Console, choose the Projects icon (under the System Configuration option) and add a project, as shown in the following graphic.

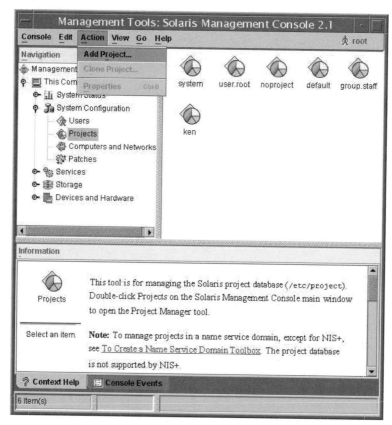

FIGURE 9-1 Selecting a System Configuration to Display

From within the project tabs, you can specify the name of the particular project you want to add. For this example, we add our e-commerce project as shown in the following graphic.

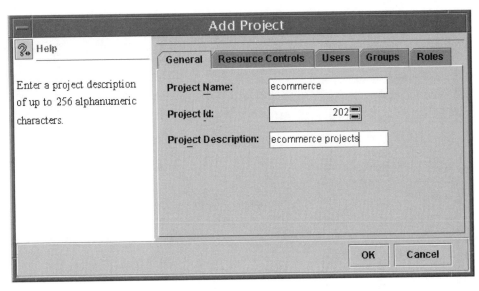

FIGURE 9-2 Selecting Projects to Display

After specifying information about the project, choose the Resource Controls tab. In the window that appears, you can impose or modify the controls on different resources such as CPU shares (called project.cpu-shares in the pull-down menu). For each resource control, you can modify:

- **Threshold.** The level at which the control activates.
- **Privilege.** Who can modify the control.
- **Signal.** What signal should be sent to processes exceeding the threshold.
- **Action.** Whether or not to deny resources to the process exceeding the threshold.

The interface displays these options as shown in the following graphic.

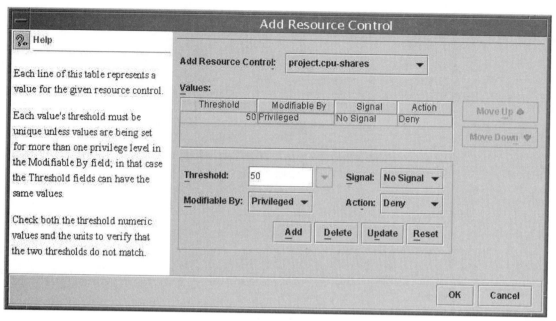

FIGURE 9-3 Modifying Controls for Resources

Accounting for resources is comparatively easy, if you have set up your categories and controls. Aside from the basic accounting (described in the assessment phase), the Solaris 9 OE also provides extended accounting. Extended accounting allows for greater access to accounting data through programmatic interfaces.

Documenting the Results

As with any project, the last thing to do on the implementation of the project is to document the results. However, you have a leg up in that department. You already have a build specification that details how the solution was installed, and you have the tools you used during the assessment phase to perform a final assessment of the environment. By reconciling the information from these two sources, document the new environment. By the end of the project, the build specification should provide the details of a new, consolidated environment.

Beyond system documentation, though, is the process documentation that you have compiled. Make sure to keep and distribute the migration process and project plans to prevent future consolidation projects from starting from scratch. Process documentation can be especially valuable if you are consolidating in "waves" as presented in Chapter 6.

Training the Administration Staff

Training is important for any new environment, but it is especially important for consolidations. With the advent of larger, more feature-filled arrays and servers, along with the added complexity of running multiple applications with a single instance of the operating environment, administrators and database administrators need to fully understand both the simple and complex operations and the choices for their new environment.

It may be difficult to decide what level of training is appropriate. A basic system administration course certainly applies, but many of the skills necessary for the environment might not be taught in these types of courses. It may be necessary to take alternative approaches to training like user group meetings, exchange programs with other companies, and even creating custom internal training.

Make sure to time the training correctly. Most studies show that without reinforcement through use on the job, newly learned skills fade within a matter of months. At Sun, we attempt to train our technical people about one month before they need the skills they learn. When skills are learned much further ahead than one month, people become "stale." When skills are learned much later, people don't have time to progress beyond the training to the more advanced topics they need to troubleshoot. Plan your training schedule accordingly.

Summary

This chapter explained how to specify the low-level details of the platform, define a migration strategy, build the consolidated environment, and deploy it. Also, it provided information about putting the solution into production, and ensuring that the administrative staff is trained and prepared to document the results of the consolidation.

Managing a Consolidated Environment

This chapter tackles some of the sticky operational issues created by the newly consolidated solution. With several applications sharing the same platform and operating system's infrastructure, availability and maintenance problems are bound to arise. However, with careful planning, strong operational processes, and flexible architectures, you can neutralize the impacts of many of these challenges.

For a variety of reasons, developing formal policies and procedures is one of the hardest things to do in a distributed computing environment. There are a variety of factors that contribute to this.

- The independent way that the UNIX world grew up provided the freedom of having your own server to develop and run applications, but also created an environment that is not conducive to formal or rigid procedures.

- Even where there is a desire for formal policies and procedures, the organizational structure often works against the operations group. Application owners and developers in the business units don't want to be bound by someone else's rules; therefore, disciplines like change control may be present in the data center, but don't extend into business units to control application development.

- Because mainframe workers, who understand policies and procedures, stayed in their half of the data center and didn't often migrate to the UNIX world, their experience with policies and procedures has not been tapped in the distributed computing environment.

The overriding issue is that the discipline to develop robust operations procedures and policies just isn't there. We need to bring some of the old "glass house" discipline back into the UNIX data center. Bringing some of the mainframe workers into the UNIX environment can be an effective way of doing this. As companies migrate applications from the mainframe to the Solaris Operating Environment, valuable people resources may become available.

We once asked a client who was in this situation whether they thought it would be more effective to teach mainframe-style discipline to the UNIX people or to teach UNIX to the mainframe people. The answer, overwhelmingly, was that it made more sense to teach UNIX to the mainframe people and to make them instrumental in implementing new policies and procedures.

This chapter provides information about the following topics:

- "Managing Availability" on page 154
- "Management Frameworks" on page 157

Managing Availability

One of the main concerns we encounter with customers is the risk of decreased availability and lower service levels in a consolidated environment. One common belief is that having each application run on its own server provides better availability. Now that we have been doing consolidation for a while, we are finding that well-run consolidated environments have substantial benefits over their predecessors and can provide increased availability. We are starting to see the analyst community agree with this position.

Over the past few years, various analysts have quoted statistics about the causes of downtime in the data center. In one of the most recent, Gartner Dataquest research showed that less than 5 percent of application downtime is attributable to disasters. Of the rest, about 40 percent is caused by application failures, performance issues, or bugs; about 40 percent by operator error, and about 20 percent by system or environmental failures, as shown in the following graphic (Gartner Measurement, February 2002). Because you can argue that the application errors are caused by people, that means that 80 percent of application downtime is related to people and the way they do their jobs. A well-managed data center with the proper policies and procedures, proper tools, and properly trained and managed people can greatly reduce the chances of application failure.

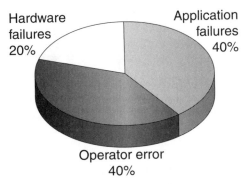

Hardware failures 20%

Application failures 40%

Operator error 40%

FIGURE 10-1 Causes of Downtime in a Data Center

While additional servers (or more precisely, additional instances of the application) might guard against some of these people and procedure problems, it will not protect you against all of them.

Identifying Potential Availability Problems

As anyone will tell you, the first step in fixing availability problems is a clear understanding of your availability expectations and the ways it will be measured. Hopefully, this situation was made clear during the assessment phase, but if it wasn't, it is not too late to correct it now. Chances are, either the expectations were clearly defined, but the measurement was undefined, or vice versa.

The first step in developing availability measurement criteria is to clearly define availability in a way that is acceptable to your customer as well as to the data center operations. This sounds obvious, but you would be amazed how often customers and operations have different definitions of availability.

Availability expectations are typically stated in Service Level Agreements (SLAs). There is certainly ample published material available on SLAs and how to write them, so we won't get into the details here. The most important factor in writing successful SLAs is that performance expectations must be clearly stated, and that the expectations must be quantifiable and measurable.

Some typical measurement criteria might include:
- Percent of application availability
- Percent of planned downtime
- Percent of unplanned downtime
- Data backup and recovery specifications
- Application recovery in case of a disaster (for example, time to recover)

There are many others, but these items are typical of what is found in most SLAs.

Note – For more information about SLAs, refer to the article "Service Level Agreement in the Data Center," by Edward Wustenhoff in the April 2002 edition of Sun BluePrints OnLine at `http://www.sun.com/solutions/blueprints/`.

With metrics in place, measuring compliance to the metrics becomes paramount. While many of the popular tools that are available can be adapted to assist your SLA-compliance monitoring, Sun has tools that are built specifically for measuring availability. The base for these tools is Sun Management Center (SunMC), Sun's monitoring suite.

SunMC provides in-depth, Sun-specific element monitoring of Sun servers. Unlike many other monitoring solutions, SunMC understands the intricacies of both the software and the hardware. For example, it allows you to view photo-realistic pictures of system hardware to identify faulty parts. Although these are impressive capabilities for supporting the system, its add-on capabilities are the most helpful for SLA measurements.

The most important add-on for SLA measurement is Configuration Service Tracker (CST) module. CST tracks:

- System availability
- System downtime
- Configuration changes

Tracking system availability and downtime can provide the vital raw data for measuring availability metrics.

Implementing Disaster Recovery

Since the September 11th tragedy in the U.S., awareness of disaster recovery has grown greatly, yet we often find that customers have not implemented any type of formal disaster recovery plan. They often rely on a simple backup and recovery strategy that is often not tested to see if it really works.

Disaster recovery is a topic that is well documented and far too extensive to detail here. Remember that disaster recovery, from the viewpoint of the data center, is part of an overall corporate discipline of business continuity. Until the business defines the level of availability, reliability, and serviceability it needs, it's difficult to implement effective disaster recovery.

One of the greatest benefits to using a consolidated approach with disaster recovery is that you have fewer servers to recover. A question you might ask yourself is whether you would rather recover 1000 servers or 100 servers. Consolidation allows you to do the latter.

Management Frameworks

As you start to develop and implement a framework for managing your consolidated data center, remember that you don't have to start from scratch. There are a variety of frameworks available to help you.

FCAPS

One commonly used framework is the International Standards Organization's FCAPS framework. FCAPS is an acronym for five levels of management of networked environments. The five levels are the fault management level (F), the configuration level (C), the accounting level (A), the performance level (P), and the security level (S). Although FCAPS was originally developed to manage networks, it is often extended to data center operations management.

At the fault management level, you can detect problems and correct them. Also, you can identify potential future problems in a proactive manner to prevent them from actually occurring.

At the configuration level, you can monitor and control data center operations. Also, you can coordinate hardware and programming changes for new, existing, and obsolete hardware and software. Asset management is also dealt with at this level.

At the accounting level, you can regulate cost controls, user account management, licenses, and other system resources.

At the performance level, you can deal with managing the overall performance of the data center. This is where application and hardware performances are monitored to maximize performance and to avoid bottlenecks.

At the security level, protect the data center from various security threats from within and from outside.

Information Technology Infrastructure Library

When you start actually writing policies and procedures, the Information Technology Infrastructure Library (ITIL) can be an invaluable resource. The British government began publishing books about best practices for information technology (IT) operations in the late 1970s. As of this writing, there are over 50 volumes available.

The ITIL has evolved and expanded to become the basis of data center management for many IT organizations, as well as by many software management tool vendors and many IT consulting groups. Many major IT consulting groups make ITIL an integral part of their data center management service offerings.

More information about ITIL can be found at http://www.itil.co.uk/.

Sun Ready Availability Assessment

In "Developing and Adhering to Well-Defined Processes" on page 21, we explained how the Sun Ready Availability Assessment (SRAA) can help assess your current infrastructure readiness for consolidation. Because Sun Professional Services (Sun PS) uses the SRAA, which is based on the FCAPS framework and utilizes material from ITIL, we will continue to focus on the SRAA as a method of implementing a robust data center management strategy.

It is important to note that in an ideal world, the majority of data center management architecture and its implementation are addressed as part of the design and implement phases. Unfortunately, this is usually not the case, and this work typically falls into the management phase.

When you look at the report that results from an SRAA, you usually find a considerable laundry list of deficiencies. Because it's virtually impossible to fix every deficiency at once, it's important to prioritize the list. In general, set priorities according to which deficiency will most negatively impact the data center's ability to deliver necessary service levels.

We generally find that the various SRAA categories should be prioritized as follows:

1. Execution management

2. Change management

3. Implementation management

4. Improvement management

5. Asset management

6. Staff management

7. Service management

8. Problem management

9. Account management

10. Program management

These may not be the correct priorities for your situation, but they are typical of what we find. Remember that these priorities do not necessarily reflect the overall level of importance of the category. They reflect the priority of typical deficiencies and the order in which we would usually attack them. For example, we give problem management a rather low priority in this ranking because most organizations have good problem management tools, policies, and procedures in place. If we simply ranked the categories, this one would certainly be one of the highest.

Execution Management

Execution management is a huge category that includes a variety of important operational areas. It includes managing, scheduling, executing, optimizing, and planning business computing processes. It also includes staff work associated with the deployment and administration of changes to the operation. Some of its major sub categories include:

- Data center operations
- Resource management
- Security
- Network management
- Business continuity

Change Management

Change management includes issues regarding the management of operational environment changes. This item is often one of the most critical categories in determining whether or not a data center will be able to deliver the necessary service levels to its customers.

In data center operations, change management is usually implemented as a four-phase life cycle, including the following phases:

- **Identification.** Uniquely identify all components of an environment.
- **Control.** Manage the process of authorizing, implementing, and documenting changes.
- **Status accounting.** Collect configuration data about the current environment.
- **Audit.** Reconcile accounting records with actual physical configuration.

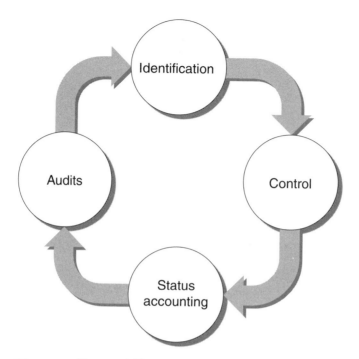

FIGURE 10-2 Phases of Change Management

A change-control board is a key element of this life cycle. The change-control board reviews, approves, and schedules all changes on the system. This centralized approach, which should encompass all stakeholders for a shared server or array, is absolutely vital to maintaining the consolidated environment.

Implementation Management

Implementation management includes the process of specifying, designing, constructing, testing, and deploying IT services. Most of this was addressed in Chapter 9. It is very important that the additional applications deployed in the consolidated environment conform to this approach. A poor deployment of a new application could cause problems across any of the shared resources.

Improvement Management

Improvement management involves managing the effectiveness, efficiency, and quality of computing services. Capacity management and planning are probably the most critical areas in this category.

Asset Management

Asset management deals with acquiring, tracking, protecting, and repairing all IT assets. This includes hardware, software, and facilities. From a consolidation viewpoint, the most important element of this category is chargeback.

One of the most common objections to consolidation is that operations will have no way to charge their customers for the use of their services and facilities. In fact, there are a variety of methods to get around this obstacle, some of which are discussed in the following paragraphs.

Many consulting groups recommend a cost-allocation scheme based on services rather than servers, but it has been difficult to clearly define how to do this. Recent developments in the Solaris 8 Operating Environment (Solaris 8 OE) and the Solaris 9 OE are starting to make service-based allocation much easier.

In the Solaris 9 OE and later versions, the implementation of server virtualization makes the saying "manage the service, not the server" a reality. The combination of Solaris Resource Manager, Solaris Containers, and Dynamic System Domains allows users to define very granular accounting and chargeback mechanisms.

In the one-application-to-one-server environment, it is easy to charge for the direct support costs and the overhead associated with a particular server. This is typically what data centers do. Most organizations have set acquisition, support, and retirement costs for the supported server and storage platforms in their data centers. For example, a Sun Fire V880 server might cost a specific amount to acquire (a fee marked up from the procurement costs to cover deployment and asset management), and might have a separate monthly fee for support and operations. While this chargeback scheme is favored by business units (it is easy to budget) and IT organizations (it is easy to administer), it does not drive maximum benefit to the organization because it promotes inefficient utilization of computing resources. A better approach would reward business units for minimizing computing resource utilization, while still being easy to administer for the IT department.

In a consolidated environment with multiple applications running on a single server, Solaris Resource Manager or the Solaris 9 Operating Environment Resource Manager can often be useful tools. Both tools allow IT staff to assign shares of an overall resource pool to an application or an application set. This share allocation can then be used to split up the cost of administering that particular server and allocate back to the customer.

There are various third-party software packages available that can help with cost allocation. One traditional vendor who has a well-known chargeback package is SAS Institute. Other vendors include those who have written billing packages for application service providers (ASPs). Many of these vendors, such as XACCT, take a network approach to cost allocation borrowed from telecommunications billing and mediation systems.

Ultimately, the concept of a utility computing model will likely be the best solution for chargeback in a consolidated environment. Utility computing has a variety of implementations, but the one most commonly requested would bill for actual compute resource usage, just as you get billed today for electricity and water.

One area of asset management that is generally not present is the use of software packages to automatically track assets. These packages have been available from vendors like Tangram, MainControl and Peregrine for several years. In the perfect world, the proper software agent would be installed on all desktops and servers before they are put into a production environment. This software allows you to periodically conduct equipment audits, and to determine the status of your server and desktop inventories.

Most of our customers do not use this type of software. Yet, when we begin working with them and ask for a list of their servers, they cannot give it to us. In general, if we have to perform a physical audit of a data center, the cost of the audit will exceed what it would have cost to deploy one of these third-party packages in the first place.

Staff Management

Staff Management includes recruiting, educating, motivating, and improving employee effectiveness and efficiency.

For consolidation, the most important element is making sure that you have the right people and that they are properly trained. If you are unsure of your staff's expertise and capabilities, take advantage of an outside evaluation service such as Sun Education's employee evaluation service to find out where you stand. Then you can easily make sure you have the proper training programs in place to eliminate any knowledge deficiencies.

Service Management

Service Management deals with the overall management of vision, strategy, architecture, and standards to implement IT services that support business goals and directions. This is generally an area that focuses on higher-level IT management rather than detailed operational levels. But on the other hand, we often find that there is no formal, high-level IT plan in place in many organizations. Ideally, high-level management formulates IT strategy and direction, and then lower-level management implements the plan and deals with tactical issues. If this high-level plan is not in place, the IT environment seems to develop in many different ways. It's almost like using a microscope to watch an amoeba grow and divide.

Problem Management

Problem Management involves the monitoring, controlling, and solving of all user problems and technology events that can impact customer Service Level Agreements. It typically includes:

- Help desk
- Escalation policies
- Internal customer relationship management

While these areas are critical to maintaining service levels, we often find that our customers already have these areas under reasonable control. If this is not the case, then the priority of this category will quickly rise to a much higher level.

Account Management

This area deals heavily with the relationship between IT and its customers. It involves the development of SLAs, and making sure that the SLA is an agreement and contract of what service expectations are and how they will be delivered. This area also deals with the reporting of results back to the customer.

This is another category that can be critical to delivering high service levels. We usually find that SLAs are adequate and in place, or that they are totally lacking. Where SLAs are lacking, we would elevate the priority of this category.

Program Management

Program management relates largely to the financial housekeeping of IT. It deals with budgets, resources, reporting, and similar tasks. It is not usually critical to managing in a consolidated environment.

One area of program management that is frequently neglected is the accounting and reporting of the people efforts and associated costs of operating the data center and of developing new software projects. Project management and project accounting should be part of the normal discipline of the data center. If it's not, it's difficult to precisely determine how your valuable people resources are being used, and whether they are being used effectively.

Summary

We cannot emphasize enough the importance of implementing a robust management structure for your data center. It can make the difference between success and failure in a consolidation project. If you don't have the time, the people, or the necessary skills to do this, get help from an organization that does.

Don't forget that the ITIL libraries are voluminous and are an excellent source of information. There are also a variety of articles available on the Internet that deal with a variety of subjects. Other people have had to work through much of this infrastructure development the hard way. Take advantage of their experience, and don't reinvent the wheel.

Sample Feasibility Study

The sample feasibility study in this appendix is the complete version of the document referenced in Chapter 5.

Introduction

Tin Can Networks' IT department requested that Sun provide assistance in determining the potential cost savings and benefits of server consolidation. The goal is to provide initial financial justification for an extensive server consolidation project across multiple data centers. To accomplish this goal, a limited feasibility study and total cost of ownership (TCO) analysis were performed.

Management Summary

This initial TCO analysis was performed using Gartner's TCO Manager software and methodology. The analysis is a simulation of expected TCO for a company of Tin Can Networks' size, in Tin Can Networks' industry and in Tin Can Networks' geographic location. The basis for this analysis is Gartner's TCO Index, a database collected from analysis of costs in over 300 data centers in over 200 companies worldwide.

The analysis was performed for three scenarios:

1. A 33 percent reduction in the number of UNIX servers

2. A 50 percent reduction in the number of UNIX servers

3. A 67 percent reduction in the number of UNIX servers

In all three cases, the analysis showed a potential substantial reduction of TCO. In each case, the potential return on investment (ROI) was favorable and indicated that the cost of implementing server consolidation was justified by the return on investment.

Business Objectives

An important factor in the success of server consolidation is to clearly identify the business objectives which TinCan hopes to achieve. During the interviews that were conducted, the following objectives were identified:

- Reduce the overall number of servers required to support manufacturing operations. This would also reduce the overall floor space needed to house the servers.
- Reduce server maintenance costs.
- Provide a computing environment that would reduce downtime and increase server availability to the manufacturing lines.
- Increase the reliability of the computing environment.
- Provide an architecture that would facilitate increased transaction volume caused by growth of the business. This growth is anticipated to be at least 50 percent over the next 12 to 18 months.

Criteria for Success

The following quantifiable success criteria were identified:

- Reduce the overall number of servers by 50 percent.
- Reduce floor space usage by 30 percent.
- Reduce server maintenance costs by 20 percent.
- Increase server availability to at least 99.9 percent.
- Increase transaction volume caused by growth of the business. This growth is anticipated to be at least 50 percent over the next 12 to 18 months.

TCO Assessment Details

The following assumptions were made for this TCO assessment:

1. The TCO analysis performed is a first-cut, rough analysis of potential savings of server consolidation.

2. The server inventory used to determine the current number of servers at Tin Can Networks was from an internal server inventory database. This database is not complete at this time. However, it was judged to be the best available source of server population information.

3. Servers included Sun, HP, and IBM.

4. Consolidation platforms were assumed to be Sun Fire 15K servers. Each server and ancillary hardware was priced at $2,000,000 per server. This price is only an estimate, and does not include any discounts or trade-ins.

5. The TCO analysis was performed using Gartner's TCO Manager software and methodology.

6. No actual costs were collected or used. All results of the simulation are based on the Gartner TCO Index, a database of TCO information derived from over 300 data centers in over 200 companies worldwide. Tin Can Networks' actual costs may differ from this model.

7. All indicated cost savings are potential. They are an indication of the types of savings that may be achieved from a server consolidation. There is no guarantee that these savings will be achieved.

Other Assumptions

Tin Can Networks background information:
- Annual revenue: $3.5 billion
- Industry: Networking hardware
- Location: Zzyzx, CA (Southwest)
- Number of employees: 20,000

The following values were used for initial and subsequent server populations. Servers are categorized based on server cost and depreciation.

	Current	Less 33%	Less 50%	Less 67%
Workgroup	285	191	143	94
Departmental	88	59	44	26
Enterprise	5	7	8	9

The following values were used for the cost of implementing server consolidation.

Note that the Additional Costs category is a general cost category that makes allowance for the inefficiencies of the consolidation process.

The following table represents a 33 percent reduction.

Less 33%	Initial	Year 1	Year 2
Server Hardware	$2,010,000	$990,000	$0
Other Hardware	$670,000	$333,000	$0
Planning & Implementation	$667,000	$333,000	$0
Additional Costs	$0	$1,000,000	$500,000

The following table represents a 50 percent reduction.

Less 50%	Initial	Year 1	Year 2
Server Hardware	$3,015,000	$1,485,000	$0
Other Hardware	$1,005,000	$495,000	$0
Planning & Implementation	$938,000	$462,000	$0
Additional Costs	$0	$1,500,000	$750,000

The following table represents a 67 percent reduction.

Less 67%	Initial	Year 1	Year 2
Server Hardware	$4,020,000	$1,980,000	$0
Other Hardware	$1,340,000	$660,000	$0
Planning and Implementation	1,206,000	$594,000	$0
Additional Costs	$0	$2,000,000	$1,000,000

Scenarios

Initially, three server consolidation scenarios were to be analyzed:

- A 33 percent reduction of the current population.
- A 50 percent reduction of the current population.
- A 67 percent reduction of the current population.

Results of TCO Analysis

The following table is a summary of scenarios one, two, and three.

TCO Analysis Overview	Current	Less 1/3	Less 1/2	Less 2/3
Direct Costs (Budgeted)				
Hardware and Software	$9,464,264	$7,119,955	$5,912,957	$4,600,926
Management	$5,887,258	$4,081,673	$3,154,821	$2,150,899
Support	$2,450,322	$1,673,731	$1,275,657	$850,389
Development	$4,405,646	$3,141,017	$2,490,969	$1,781,631
Communications	$2,903,170	$2,053,642	$1,617,797	$1,152,403
Direct Costs	$25,110,660	$18,070,017	$14,452,200	$10,536,247

TCO Analysis Overview	Current	Less 1/3	Less 1/2	Less 2/3
Indirect Costs (Unbudgeted)				
End-User IS Costs	$0	$0	$0	$0
Downtime	$1,182,152	$824,833	$641,355	$442,246
Indirect Costs	$1,182,152	$824,833	$641,355	$442,246
Annual Total Cost of Ownership (TCO)	$26,292,812	$18,894,850	$15,093,555	$10,978,493
Annual TCO per User	$0	$0	$0	$0
Annual TCO per Client	$0	$0	$0	$0
Annual TCO per Asset	$69,558	$73,521	$77,403	$85,105
TCO as a Percentage of Annual Revenue	0.70%	0.50%	0.40%	0.30%
Direct Costs as a Percentage of Annual Revenue	0.70%	0.50%	0.40%	0.30%
Management Staff FTEs	30.9	21.5	20.1	11.5
Users per Network, Systems, and Storage Management FTE	0	0	0	0
FTE Operations and Support Staff	8	5.5	5.2	2.8

The following is a graphical representation of the summary results of this table.

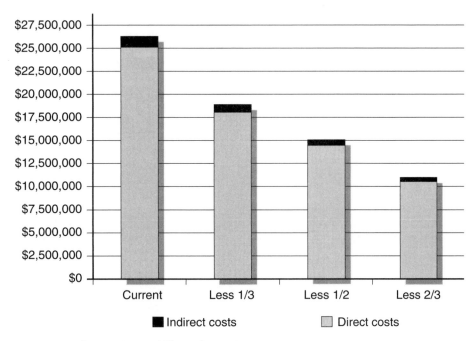

FIGURE A-1 Comparison of Three Scenarios

Here, the effect of server consolidation on TCO can be seen more dramatically. This indicates that there is a clear advantage to consolidation.

ROI Analysis: Scenario One

The following table shows the ROI analysis for scenario one.

ROI Analysis—Typical vs. Target	Initial	Year 1	Year 2	Year 3	Total
Implementation Costs	$3,334,000	$2,666,000	$500,000	$0	$6,500,000
Cumulative Implementation Costs	$3,334,000	$6,000,000	$6,500,000	$6,500,000	
Net Present Value (NPV) of Project Implementation	$6,112,954				
TCO—Typical	n/a	$164,368,805	$164,368,805	$164,368,805	$493,106,415.00
TCO—Target	n/a	$156,970,844	$156,970,844	$156,970,844	$470,912,531
Implementation Rollout	n/a	67%	33%	0%	100%
Adjusted TCO—Target		$159,412,171	$156,970,844	$156,970,844	$473,353,858
Projected Savings	n/a	$4,956,634	$7,397,961	$7,397,961	$19,752,557
Economic Benefits		$0	$0	$0	$0
Savings plus Benefits	n/a	$4,956,634	$7,397,961	$7,397,961	$19,752,557
Cumulative Savings plus Benefits	0	$4,956,634	$12,354,596	$19,752,557	
Cash Flow	($3,334,000)	$2,290,634	$6,897,961	$7,397,961	$13,252,557
Cumulative Cash Flow	($3,334,000)	($1,043,366)	$5,854,596	$13,252,557	

ROI Analysis—Typical vs. Target	Initial	Year 1	Year 2	Year 3	Total
Cost of Funds	12%				
Net Present Value (NPV) of Project Cash Flow	$9,475,945				
Internal Rate of Return (IRR)	114%				

The following is a graphical representation of this ROI analysis of scenario one.

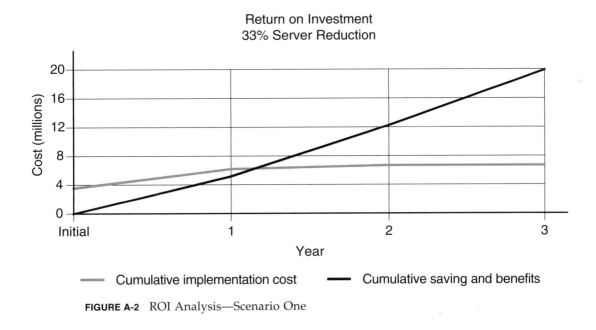

FIGURE A-2 ROI Analysis—Scenario One

ROI Analysis: Scenario Two

The following table shows the ROI analysis for scenario two.

ROI Analysis—Typical vs. Target	Initial	Year 1	Year 2	Year 3	Total
Implementation Costs	$4,958,000	$3,942,000	$750,000	$0	$9,650,000
Cumulative Implementation Costs	$4,958,000	$8,900,000	$9,650,000	$9,650,000	
Net Present Value (NPV) of Project Implementation	$9,075,538				
TCO—Typical	n/a	$164,368,805	$164,368,805	$164,368,805	$493,106,415
TCO—Target	n/a	$153,169,548	$153,169,548	$153,169,548	$459,508,645
Implementation Rollout	n/a	67%	33%	0%	100%
Adjusted TCO—Target		$156,865,303	$153,169,548	$153,169,548	$463,204,400
Projected Savings	n/a	$7,503,502	$11,199,257	$11,199,257	$29,902,015
Economic Benefits		$0	$0	$0	$0
Savings plus Benefits	n/a	$7,503,502	$11,199,257	$11,199,257	$29,902,015
Cumulative Savings plus Benefits	n/a	$7,503,502	$18,702,759	$29,902,015	
Cash Flow	($4,958,000)	$3,561,502	$10,449,257	$11,199,257	$20,252,015
Cumulative Cash Flow	($4,958,000)	($1,396,498)	$9,052,759	$20,252,015	
Cost of Funds	12%				
Net Present Value (NPV) of Project Cash Flow	$14,523,406				
Internal Rate of Return (IRR)	117%				

The following is a graphical representation of this ROI analysis of scenario two.

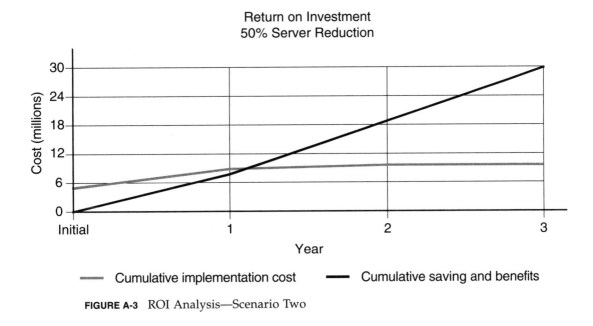

FIGURE A-3 ROI Analysis—Scenario Two

ROI Analysis: Scenario Three

The following table shows the ROI analysis for scenario three.

ROI Analysis—Typical vs. Target	Initial	Year 1	Year 2	Year 3	Total
Implementation Costs	$6,566,000	$5,234,000	$1,000,000	$0	$12,800,000
Cumulative Implementation Costs	$6,566,000	$11,800,000	$12,800,000	$12,800,000	
Net Present Value (NPV) of Project Implementation	$12,036,408				
TCO—Typical	n/a	$164,368,805	$164,368,805	$164,368,805	$493,106,415
TCO—Target	n/a	$149,054,487	$149,054,487	$149,054,487	$447,163,460
Implementation Rollout	n/a	60%	40%	0%	100%

ROI Analysis—Typical vs. Target	Initial	Year 1	Year 2	Year 3	Total
Adjusted TCO—Target		$155,180,214	$149,054,487	$149,054,487	$453,289,187
Projected Savings	n/a	$9,188,591	$15,314,318	$15,314,318	$39,817,228
Economic Benefits		$0	$0	$0	$0
Savings Plus Benefits	n/a	$9,188,591	$15,314,318	$15,314,318	$39,817,228
Cumulative Savings Plus Benefits	n/a	$9,188,591	$24,502,909	$39,817,228	
Cash Flow	($6,566,000)	$3,954,591	$14,314,318	$15,314,318	$27,017,228
Cumulative Cash Flow	($6,566,000)	($2,611,409)	$11,702,909	$27,017,228	
Cost of Funds	12%				
Net Present Value (NPV) of Project Cash Flow	$19,276,601				
Internal Rate of Return (IRR)	114%				

The following is a graphical representation of this ROI analysis of scenario three.

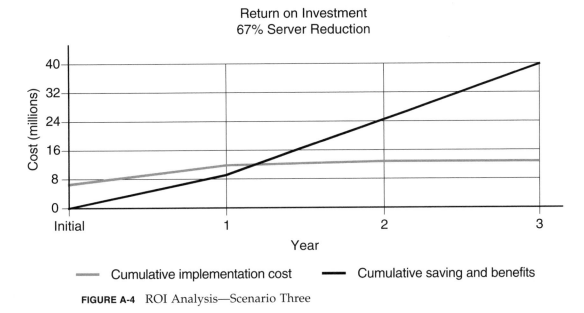

FIGURE A-4   ROI Analysis—Scenario Three

Conclusions

Based on these preliminary analyses of the various scenarios, both TCO and ROI strongly support this server consolidation project. Increasingly aggressive levels of consolidation should produce increased savings for Tin Can Networks.

Sample Application Profile

This appendix presents a sample application profile for a fictitious company, Acme Corporation.

Revision Information

The following revision information applies to the Acme Corporation application profile.

Title	PeopleSoft HRMS			
Subject	Requirement Definition, Requirements Collection, Requirements Management			
Author(s)	Jane Doe			
Application Owner & Contact Info	Jane Doe, 312-556-2543, jane.doe@acme.com			
Date	5/5/02			
Company	Acme Corporation			
Revision Number	**Date**	**Revision Author**	**Revision Description (Changes)**	
0.1	5/19	Tracy Lauren	Add new sections to enhance information gathering	
0.2	5/19	Jim Woods	Copied Tracyís revs into development & test sections	
0.3	5/26	Jim Woods	Cleaned up filesystem info; added kernel config info	

FIGURE B-1   Revision Information for Acme Corporation

Application

PeopleSoft Human Resources Management Software (HRMS) contains three core modules: Human Resources, Base Benefits, and Payroll Interface. The application version is 7.5 and the tools version is 7.54.10. We will be applying a new application version of 7.51, prior to the go-live date. The HRMS application is the core system supporting 5000 employees of the Acme Corporation. Future plans include adding Latin American operations and other lines of business. The HRMS system includes Online Transaction Processing (OLTP), batch, and reporting.

Production Environment

The following information describes the production environment for the Acme Corporation.

End-User Overview

128 base users, no priority users; 50 percent concurrent users.

System Uptime Requirements

Uptime is 24/7, except Sundays from 7:00 a.m. to 12:00 p.m. MST, and Saturday evenings from 9:00 p.m. until 11:00 p.m. MST.

End-User Log In

End users *must* be able to log in during the hours of 5:00 a.m. MST to 9:00 p.m. MST, Monday through Friday.

Batch Cycles

Batch cycles will run during the hours of midnight to 5:00 a.m. MST.

Sign On During Batch Cycles

Users will be allowed to sign on during batch cycles, but users are aware of the possible consequences.

Maintenance Windows

The maintenance window is 7:00 a.m. to 12:00 p.m. MST each Sunday. Backups occur from 9:00 p.m. to approximately 11:00 p.m. MST each evening. These are hot backups. System backup and cold backups are performed Saturday evening 9:00 p.m. to 11:00 p.m MST.

Dependencies—Application Interfaces

HPRD will have a link to FPRD (PeopleSoft Financials Production). The following table lists all interfaces between this application and other systems.

TABLE B-1   Interfaces Between Application and Other Systems

Common Name Used to Refer to Interface	Interface Type Flat File or Sqlnet Access to Database	Transmission Mechanism FTP, Network, Internet, Other	Send or Receive Data	UNIX Accounts for Transmissions *Please note proxy accounts used*	Description and Comments
From PS HRMS to payroll interface	Flat file	FTP—need to get account transfer and/or FTP.	Initiated by clerk as needed.	New, setup.	Interface for flat files sent and received from the payroll product and PS HRMS; stored in $PSHOME.
HR to financial	Sqlnet access	Network	Receives/ views; initiated by HRMS.	Not applicable.	An SQL view that is used during a drop-down box selection.
Kronos	Flat file	FTP—need to get account transfer and/or FTP.	Sends/receives.	Need to get account.	Files are sent and received from the Kronos application to the client. The Kronos application remains on the old hardware because the version is not Sun certified.

Performance Requirements

The following information describes the performance requirements for the Acme Corporation.

Expected Typical User Response Time

The batch processing goal is less than two minutes.

Batch Processing Window

The batch window has not been defined yet, but these are the probable jobs to be executed. The time will be from 12:00 a.m. to 6:00 a.m. MST.

TABLE B-2 Batch Processing Window

Payroll interface	Cobol
Security update	Sqr
Employees update	Sqr
Deduction Calculations	Cobol

Peak Processing Periods

Peak processing will be Monday and Tuesday of each week, with Tuesday being the highest. Payroll is actually run on Tuesday and transmitted to ADP. Payroll Interface will, more than likely, be run on Monday nights. Morning hours (8:00 a.m. to noon) on Tuesday are the peak hours.

Current Server Operation Overview

This is a new application, with no current server. (Please provide the equivalent information planned for the production environment.)

Monitoring Needs

The following table identifies monitoring needs, with "N/A" by those that don't apply.

TABLE B-3   Monitoring Needs for Acme Corporation

Type of Monitoring	Third-Party Tools/Custom Tools	Scope of Monitoring
Database monitoring.	Custom scripts that are tied into Openview ITO, Openview plug in for Oracle (DB-SPI?)	Statistics and errors
Application monitoring	Process monitoring; log file monitoring	Currently not being done (out of scope); but would be nice
Network monitoring	Server ping	N/A
Operating system monitoring (including key application-specific resources)	Openview, ITO	N/A

Network and Infrastructure Services Used by Application

List all network and infrastructure services used by the application.

Naming Service Requirements

The naming service requirements are as follows:
- DNS
- Oracle Names Service (or TNSNAMES files).
- We only use TNSNAMES for developers and implementation analysts, and among the servers themselves. All 14 users of the system log in using TCP/IP and Tuxedo ports.
- The Tnsnames.ora file is replicated and distributed among the database servers through the rsync command, or a similar command.

Project Constraints

July is a constraint due to the new application go-live date. We would like to have the new production HRMS environment built by June 15th for testing conversion programs and performance, if possible.

Security Requirements

The primary requirement is inside the firewall. We allow dial-up access through RAS and the use of the Microsoft Windows Terminal Server.

Application Failover Configuration Requirements

If this application has a failover mechanism, describe it, provide the maximum elapsed time for failover, and define the scope.

- Not applicable for PeopleSoft

Prerequisite Software Components

The following table identifies prerequisite software components, including middleware, for Acme Corporation.

TABLE B-4   Prerequisite Software Components for Acme Corporation

Product	Vendor	Version	Configuration
Tuxedo	Beasys	6.4	PeopleSoft delivers several pre-programmed server processes. With HRMS, these consist of: • PSAUTH (authenticates operator IDs and passwords) • PSQCKSRV (runs nonconversational client requests [short services]) • PSAPPSRV (runs nonconversational client requests [long services]) • PSSAMSRV (runs conversational client requests) • PSAPISRV (supports the message agent calls) • PSQRYSRV (dedicated service to ad hoc queries) Each server process contains detail services, which perform the requests from the client. The PeopleSoft configuration tools allow you to choose how many of these server processes to launch, depending on our user counts. The configuration is based on user counts and PeopleSoft recommendations. Domain HPRD1-psauth (1/2), psappsrv (3/5), psqcksrv (4/6), psapisrv (1/1), pssamsrv (1/3), psqrysrv (4/6). This domain will be our main processor, and is sized using the medium model (100-1000 users). Domain HPRD2-psauth (1/1), psappsrv (1/2), psqcksrv (1/2), psapisrv (1/1), pssamsrv (1/2), psqrysrv (2/3). This domain is mainly used by application support and is sized using the small module. (1–100 users) Enviroment variables: (to be on new domain) ORACLEHOME=/oracle/product/7.3.4 Note: Finance utilizes version 6.3
Jolt	Beasys	1.1 v2	N/A

TABLE B-4   Prerequisite Software Components for Acme Corporation *(Continued)*

Product	Vendor	Version	Configuration

SQR	Scribe	4.2.3	Enviroment Variables: (to be on new domain)
			`ESQDIR=/apps/sqr432/ora/bin`
			`SQRDIR=/apps/sqr432/ora/bin`
			`SQRBIN=/apps/sqr432/ora/bin`
			`SQRTOOLS=/apps/sqr432/ora/bin`
			`ESQREDITOR=vi`
			Directory paths used
			Operating System Account used by SQR
			
			Note: Finance utilizes version 3.0.18.

Oracle	Oracle	7.3.4.3	On UNIX, with Oracle 7.3.x, there are some Oracle installation options that are incompatible with the PeopleSoft product. Specifically, advanced networking options (ANO), the SPX/IPX protocol adapter, and the NIS naming adapter. When installing the Oracle RDBMS on your database server, do not select the aforementioned options. Currently, PeopleSoft supports only the default Oracle date format of DD-MON-YY. They have written their date conversion code to expect the DD-MON-YY format. However, although this shows a two-digit year, PeopleSoft provides the appropriate masking of the dates to include a four-digit year.
COBOL compiler	Micro Focus	4.1	Note: The MicroFocus compiler for COBOL may be the only COBOL supported compiler with PeopleSoft Note: The COBOL paths listed may be referencing the HP COBOL compiler/libraries (`cecoux15`)

Kernel Configuration Changes

We have combination kernel parameters for groups of applications, but not for each application.

Kernel parameters for PeopleSoft Suite (includes PeopleSoft Financials, Oracle 7.4.3.1, HRMS, Tuxedo 6.3/6.4, SQR 3.0.18/4.3).

```
*Shared memory parameters
        set  shmsys:shminfo_shmmin=1
        set  shmsys:shminfo_shmmax=3221225472
        set  shmsys:shminfo_shmmni=512
        set  shmsys:shminfo_shmseg=512

*Semaphore parameters
        set  semsys:seminfo_semmap=6322
        set  semsys:seminfo_semmni=6322
        set  semsys:seminfo_semmns=71680
        set  semsys:seminfo_semmnu=1024
        set  semsys:seminfo_semmsl=500
        set  semsys:seminfo_semume=100
        set  semsys:seminfo_semopm=50

*Message queue parameters
        set  msgsys:msginfo_msgmap=32767
        set  msgsys:msginfo_msgmax=48000
        set  msgsys:msginfo_msgmnb=65536
        set  msgsys:msginfo_msgmni=16000
        set  msgsys:msginfo_msgssz=128
        set  msgsys:msginfo_msgtql=7548
        set  msgsys:msginfo_msgseg=32767
```

Miscellaneous

The following information describes the database sizing information, portability issues, and existing deficiencies for the Acme Corporation.

Database Sizing Information

- Number of employee records in HR database: 6700 active, 16,000 total records including terminations.
- Estimated size of the HR database (used/allocated): 5 gigabyte/10 gigabyte

Portability Issues

Identify custom-written programs or shell scripts that may require porting effort due to non-ANSI C compliance, HP-specific UNIX commands, and HP-specific compiler option used.

- Custom shell script $PS_HOME/bin/opr_print. This script is used to retrieve the operator-specific printer name for SQR printing. The script is called from prcs_sqr in the bin directory.

Existing Deficiencies

Identify existing deficiencies or nonfunctioning aspects of the application or environment.

- Currently, the application is experiencing some type of corruption related to the PeopleSoft %date function. The result is that default panel dates are populated incorrectly.
- The Microsoft Windows Terminal Server environment does not provide the end-user access to the networked H drive. Not a pertinent issue to this project. The issue will be resolved by the network group.
- Can you print Crystal reports through the Microsoft Windows Terminal Server? The issues we experience today with Crystal software are related to the installation. When you have both financials and HRMS installed on the desktop, Crystal will link to the most recent installation. This error occurs in the Microsoft Windows Terminal Server and the client. PeopleSoft does not have a fix for this problem. We recommend you reinstall between switching applications. We do not have printing issues from the Microsoft Windows Terminal Server or the client.

Printing Architecture

Provide an overview of the application's printing architecture. Identify all software components needed to install and manage the planned production printing subsystem (for example, include JetAdmin and version).

- May use JetAdmin; current version on `cecoux21` is: Version D.01.08
- Expected to need only standard lp services.
- Need to identify all HRMS locations and the necessary printer queues. These will need to be set up on the server for SQR printing.
- Print queues on `cecoux21` are `21105_1_is`, `24401_1_is`, `24901_1_is`, `24901_1_is_1`, `32204_1_acct`, `acctae_print`, `cehqop01`, `cetugl_print`, `cscitrix_print`, `drc_central`, `istsprt`, `usdcrpgl_print`.
- Custom print filters used by this application: None.

Network Architecture

List all networking protocols, or networking services used by this application and its prerequisite software. (This information was provided by the network group.)

- TCP/IP: Yes.
- SQLNet (Oracle): Yes.
- LPR/LPD (printing): Unknown.
- FTP (interfaces perhaps): Yes.

Detailed TCP/IP Port Requirements

The following table lists all application-specific TCP/IP port allocation requirements. If applicable include any nonstandard port numbers used for standard TCP/IP services.

- Not determined for HRMS. We use financials established ports as a guide.

Note – The TNSLSNR 1521/TCP (listener port) is found in the file /etc/services and /oracle/product/7.3.2/network/admin/tnsnames.ora (on the cecoux21).

TABLE B-5 TCP/IP Port Allocation Requirements

Application Component	Starting Port # if Range	Ending Port # if Range	Static or Dynamic	Comments
Tuxedo Domain A WSL Listener			Static	
Tuxedo Domain A WHL range			Dynamic	
Tuxedo Domain B WSL Listener			Static	
Tuxedo Domain B WHL range			Dynamic	
Tuxedo Domain C WSL Listener			Static	
Tuxedo Domain C WHL range			Dynamic	
HRMS Production Database Oracle Port			Static	
Maestro				
Oracle NetBackup				
Performance Tools?				
Licensing Tools?				

File System Requirements

List any application-specific file system requirements. For example, in order to maximize I/O performance with VERITAS file services (vxfs), and Oracle, the block size of the vxfs should match the Oracle block size.

■ Sample fstab and script used to create vxfs would be helpful.

■ Directories for HRMS will follow the same standard as in development. No special requirements exist.

- File system naming conventions are: /psft/hr (for PeopleSoft HRMS), and /psft/fs (for PeopleSoft Financials)

Hardware Requirements

The following information describes the hardware requirements for the Acme Corporation.

Storage Requirements

Estimates based on our conversion database size are 5 gigabytes used, and 10 gigabytes allocated.

TABLE B-6   Storage Requirements

Volume	Hyper Information	Size/Used	Mount Point	RAID	FS Type	Backup	Purpose
PeopleSoft			/psft/hr/hprd		vxfs for all		HRMS production
Oracle databases					vxfs for all		
Tuxedo			/tuxedo6.4		vxfs for all		Version 6.4
SQR			/apps/sqr423		vxfs for all		Version 4.2.3
MicroFocus COBOL			/opt/cobol_4.0		vxfs for all		

Note – Currently the /psft directory for finance on server15 is not mirrored, and is on the vxfs file system.

Network Requirements

Network requirements are unknown at this time.

CPU Requirements

CPU requirements are unknown at this time.

Memory Requirements

Memory requirements are unknown at this time.

Other Requirements

Printer drivers for printing SQR output from the UNIX server to the network printer.

Non-UNIX Infrastructure Components

Provide architectural-level configuration information pertaining to this application. (PeopleSoft includes all batch servers, also known as process schedulers, all file servers, clients, Microsoft Windows Terminal Servers.)

- Payroll software will run on a Microsoft Windows NT server and provide flat files to the HRMS.

- The Microsoft Windows Terminal Server will run on a Microsoft Windows NT server, and allows remote access to the application for support personnel.

- No other PeopleSoft components run outside of UNIX (for example, process schedulers).

Glossary

air gap   Two or more networks that are physically unconnected. This is a security mechanism that prevents unauthorized access in the network.

architecture   The specific design and components of a computer system, and the way they interact with one another.

archive   A collection of several files bundled into one file by a program for shipment or storage.

backward consolidation   Consolidations of existing applications.

begin script   A Bourne shell script specified in the JumpStart server `rules` file that is executed before a Solaris Operating Environment installation begins.

boot block   An 8-Kbyte disk block that contains information used to boot a system. The boot block directly follows the disk label.

boot server   A system that provides the services and information necessary to boot an installation client.

business tier   The tier where applications or middleware run in conjunction with the other tiers. See also presentation tier and resource tier.

client-server architecture   A distributed computing architecture where one system, the server, provides information and services to another system, the client.

configuration   Software options that tell computer system components how to operate.

configuration server   A system that provides the client its unique profile and software configuration. This server specifies partition sizes, the list of software to install, begin and finish scripts, etc.

daemon   A process that runs in the background, handling commands delivered for local or remote command execution.

default   A value, attribute, or option used when none has been specified.

demand-only connection	Simple security measure accomplished by removal of JumpStart entries when installation is complete.
dependent keyword	A word that specifies additional configuration details that may be required by a service or facility. Always associated with an independent keyword.
device driver	The software that converts device-independent requests into device-specific (or device-dependent) commands.
DHCP	Dynamic Host Configuration Protocol. A standard to automatically and dynamically provide an IP address to a client. One of the ways to provide a JumpStart client with its IP address.
direct costs	Capital, fees, and labor costs spent by the corporate IT department, business units, and departmental IT groups to deliver IT services and solutions. Costs include hardware and software expenses, information systems operations labor, service desk labor, information systems finance and administration labor, outsourced management, and support fees.
disaster recovery	The planning and provision of data center services under any circumstances, even during a natural disaster such as flood or earthquake. Also referred to as Business Continuity Planning.
DNS	Domain Name System. An Internet standard service for the association and lookup of host names and IP addresses.
driver script	A script used to control the execution of multiple begin or finish scripts.
encapsulation	The method by which the Veritas Volume Manager (VxVM) software takes over management of a disk that has data that must be preserved.
FCAPS	An acronym for five levels of management of networked environments, including fault management (F), configuration (C), accounting (A), performance (P), and security (S). Although FCAPS was originally developed to manage networks, it is often extended to data center operations management.
feasibility study	A document that defines the business objectives and the expected results of the project. This document states the project scope, simulates the expected reduction in total cost of ownership (TCO), and simulates the expected return on investment (ROI).
forward consolidation	The development of new applications in a consolidated environment.
FTP	File Transfer Protocol. FTP, which is based on TCP/IP, enables the fetching and storing of files between hosts on the Internet. See also TCP/IP
granularity	The level of detail at which something is being considered or examined.
HTTP	Hypertext Transport Protocol. The Internet standard that fetches hypertext objects from remote hosts.

independent keyword	A word that fully designates a service or facility and does not require a dependent keyword to provide additional configuration specifications.
install server	The source of software packages that are to be installed on the client.
installation client	The system on which the Solaris Operating Environment is to be installed. The installation client can be any hardware platform capable of running the Solaris Operating Environment, including those hardware platforms typically referred to as servers.
interactive installation	An installation of the Solaris Operating Environment done manually, with interaction from the person installing the system.
indirect costs	Costs that measure the efficiency of IT to deliver expected services to end users, and the extent to which end users are likely to be burdened with self-support, peer support, and downtime.
IP address	A unique 32-bit number that identifies each host on a TCP/IP network.
ITIL	Information Technology Infrastructure Library. The library created by the British government for books about best practices for information technology (IT) operations.
kernel	The core of the operating system software. The kernel is the lowest software level and runs directly on the hardware. The kernel manages all system resources and implements fundamental software services, such as virtual memory management, that the hardware may not provide.
keyword	A specific or predefined word or phrase in a document or record that is used in accessing, sorting, or searching.
LAN	Local area network.
LDAP	Lightweight Directory Access Protocol. A name service.
logical consolidation	Implementing standards and best practices across a server population to manage the environment more efficiently and effectively.
man pages	UNIX online documentation.
n-tier architecture	An architecture where various components of the application are separated and run on specialized servers.
name services	In a general sense, a repository that organizes and names objects. It provides an association, often referred to as a binding, between a name and an object.
NAS	Network attached storage.
network segmentation	A security mechanism that uses a physically separated network to isolate network traffic.

NFS	Network file system. Sun's distributed computing file system.
NIS	Network Information Service. Sun Microsystems' distributed name service.
NIS+	Network Information Service Plus. A hierarchical name repository that is a successor to NIS.
N-tier architectures	A datacenter architecture where well-defined system types are provided in tiers. N-Tier architectures permit segmentation of servers.
OBP	OpenBoot PROM (programmable read-only memory). The system firmware.
OS	Operating system. Acollection of programs that control the use of the hardware and supervise the other programs executed by the system.
patches	Updates and enhancements to the Solaris Operating Environment or application software.
physical consolidation	Consolidating data centers and moving servers to fewer physical locations.
presentation tier	This tier is usually comprised of several small, one or two processor servers running UNIX, Linux, or Windows. See also business tier and resource tier.
rationalization	The deployment of multiple applications on fewer, larger servers and in fewer instances of the operating system (OS).
resource profiles	Sets of skills required to accomplish specific tasks within a project plan.
resource tier	Usually thought of as the heart of the data center, this tier is characterized by large, scalable servers that run mission-critical applications and databases. See also business tier and presentation tier.
ROI	Return on investment. The benefit you receive from a consolidation.
SAN	Storage area network. Technology that inserts a network, or fabric, of switching devices between servers and storage that enable any server or application to access any storage connected to it. The fabric can then be configured to allow various servers to access various storage.
snapshot	A point-in-time copy of a system or disk.
staging environment	A network environment used for the prebuiliding, burn-in, testing, and integration testing of systems and services before the systems and services are moved to their appropriate location on the network.
TCO	Total cost of ownership. A concept largely developed by Gartner over the last few years, TCO is the methodology used by Sun Professional Services. It focuses on the costs of an IT environment.
TCP/IP	Transmission Control Protocol/Internet Protocol. An Internet protocol that provides for the reliable delivery of data streams from one host to another. SunOS networks run on TCP/IP by default.

validate   To have an application verify that the contents of a text field are appropriate to the function.

VLAN   Virtual local area network.

VxVM   VERITAS Volume Manager.

WAN   Wide area network. A network consisting of many distributed systems. This network can cover a large physical area, sometimes worldwide.

Index

horizontal scaling
    defined, 119
    example, 120

W

informIT

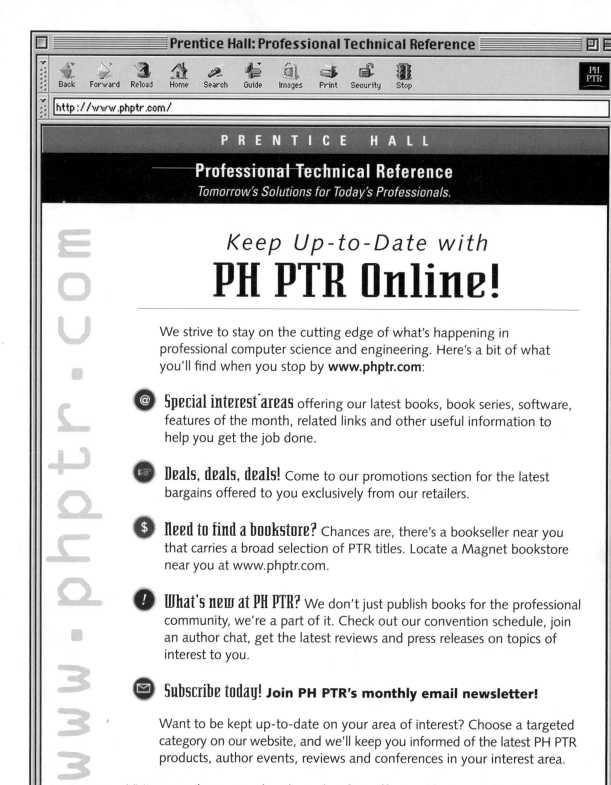